COMING
ABOUT

DAVID PARAGAMIAN

COMING ABOUT

HOW WE TRANSFORMED A MAJOR MEDIA COMPANY AND THE LESSONS THERE FOR YOU

Advantage | Books

Published by Advantage, Charleston, South Carolina.
Member of Advantage Media.

ADVANTAGE is a registered trademark, and the Advantage colophon is a trademark of Advantage Media Group, Inc.

Printed in the United States of America.

10 9 8 7 6 5 4 3 2 1

ISBN: 9781642256819 (Hardcover)
ISBN: 9781642256802 (eBook)

LCCN: 2022921186

Cover design by Analisa Smith.
Layout design by David Taylor.

This publication is designed to provide accurate and authoritative information in regard to the subject matter covered. It is sold with the understanding that the publisher is not engaged in rendering legal, accounting, or other professional services. If legal advice or other expert assistance is required, the services of a competent professional person should be sought.

Advantage Media helps busy entrepreneurs, CEOs, and leaders write and publish a book to grow their business and become the authority in their field. Advantage authors comprise an exclusive community of industry professionals, idea-makers, and thought leaders. Do you have a book idea or manuscript for consideration? We would love to hear from you at **AdvantageMedia.com**.

This book is for everyone facing obstacles, challenges, and things they simply want to change and improve. May this book unlock the "gift of the pivot" for you.

CONTENTS

INTRODUCTION

Change is hard. Ask anyone who is trying to lose weight or go to school at night while they work all day. Not impossible. Just hard. And true transformation—well, that's harder still. But people do transform in meaningful ways. Even institutions, like colleges, can transform. I know. I went to a school that transformed from an all-male institution to a much better coed institution. And companies, when faced with critical turning points, can pivot and transform too.

The business landscape, though, is littered with companies that couldn't make the pivot. When faced with a critical strategic moment, they just didn't make it—whether due to old strategies or outdated day-to-day execution approaches. We know those companies that, once mighty, are now gone. Think about Kodak. For years, every Academy Award–winning movie was shot on Kodak film. Then the digital pivot came—and Kodak missed it. Or think about Blackberry. There was a time when the Blackberry was *the* indispensable business tool. But then competition arrived from the iPhone, and, today, Blackberry is essentially gone. These are companies that couldn't make the transformational pivot.

But great organizations *can* make the pivot. In this book, I want to share how a great forty-year-old media company, the Health

Monitor Network, made the pivot from a legacy print media company to an industry-leading, modern digital marketing platform.

But let me start with my personal story of change—because, you see, I know the trials of transformation firsthand. For much of my early life, I was averse to change. I was the kid who colored inside the lines, literally. I had a great respect for the rules. As I got older, I considered going to the Naval Academy, where I felt I would get that high level of structure and discipline I loved.

I didn't end up taking that path, but I carried that mindset into early adulthood. In keeping with that ethos, my career began on a traditional track, working for big-name companies that had rooted their success in consistency—Procter & Gamble, Roche Pharmaceuticals, and Publicis Groupe, to name just a few.

Then, as happens in life, I was thrown a curveball.

In a short span of time, I found myself eulogizing my mother, my father, and my wife. It was a period that I wouldn't wish on my worst enemy. To say it shook me is an understatement. My entire existence, I had pursued a clear path and envisioned a certain life for myself, both personally and professionally. I certainly never envisioned myself being a single parent with three kids—two daughters in college and a high school–aged son at home.

> **In a short span of time, I found myself eulogizing my mother, my father, and my wife. It was a period that I wouldn't wish on my worst enemy.**

When your life is altered that drastically, you start to question some of your old practices and modes of thought. For me, my adherence to the traditional rules of life (as I had conceived them in all the "wisdom" of youth) came under scrutiny. Consider this: my wife had never picked up a cigarette a day in her life, and she died from lung cancer.

We had played by the rules, if you will, and where had it gotten us?

That period in which I had change thrust upon me was, ironically enough, when my deep love of transformation was born. Now I have a great appreciation for change. I've spent more than thirty years of my career as a change agent, working in executive roles to spur transformation, build sustainable leadership teams, and drive revenue.

Health Monitor, where I currently serve as CEO, epitomizes the greatness that positive change can bring. A legacy historical print media business, the company was disproportionately hit by the COVID-19 pandemic. Internal changes (like employees shifting to telework) coincided with massive external upheaval (like revenues declining, as advertisers—reluctant to invest in print publications for empty physicians' waiting rooms—hit pause).

Health Monitor faced an urgent need to pivot and transition to a fully twenty-first-century digital platform. And it did just that. But it took time, effort, and—above all—a team of very determined people to make it happen.

From my experiences at Health Monitor and before, I've come to recognize that the inspiration for change doesn't always come from sunny mornings and clear skies. In fact, it usually comes from just the opposite—the tough times. But if we have the grit to push through those tough times, to stay standing through those moments of upheaval, we can come out on the other side better, stronger, and—if we're in it with some good people—grateful for the experience.

Change Takes Time: Playing by the Rules at P&G

I did not always feel this kind of gratitude for change. When I was younger, the last thing I wanted was to shake things up. My very first job out of college was with Procter & Gamble (P&G), the global king of consumer packaged goods—and a company noted for its (highly successful) by-the-book approach.

I vividly remember how shocked and flattered I was when P&G recruited me on the Hamilton College campus. I was having lunch with some friends—munching away on a tuna sandwich—when the district sales manager for Buffalo, New York, approached me and said, "What do I have to do to get you to interview with me?" I was floored. Through a mouthful of tuna, I stuttered out an answer, telling him I would do anything to work for P&G—but that I wanted to be in marketing, not sales. After flying to Cincinnati for an interview, that's where I ended up.

P&G was all about rigor, training, and rules. I loved it. In a way, P&G was the Naval Academy that I never got to go to. They were the quintessential paint-by-numbers kind of company, and they whipped me into shape, fine-tuning my speaking, writing, and overall presentation skills—all according to their well-trodden formula for success.

Their mindset at that time was this: "There's a way to do things, and we're going to teach you that way." They even had an acronym for it: CBA—current best approach. Based on their extensive experience and rigorous data analysis, they had identified what worked for building brands and consumer promotion. They had their CBA, and everything (and everyone) aligned with it.

P&G was where I cut my teeth—first in marketing and later in the sales division—and, logically, their regimented approach spoke to me. From there, I continued on a pretty traditional career path, climbing the proverbial ladder, often working for companies built on long-standing tradition—companies with clear rule books. And I played by the rules. I wasn't one to shy away from the truth, but I also wasn't one to ruffle feathers. That would eventually change—starting with my experience at Razorfish Health.

Change Requires Telling Difficult Truths: Turning around Razorfish Health

In my earlier days, a work friend nicknamed me the Senator for my diplomacy skills. He said that, like a good senator, I could stake out both sides of any argument: it could be this, *or* it could be that. That's an identity I shed after losing three loved ones—my parents and my wife—in a short period of time. That experience forced me to change, and it's a change I brought forward with me in both my professional and my personal life.

Seeking a fresh start, in 2015, I went to work for Publicis Groupe, the Paris-based holding company of multiple advertising, media, and public relations agencies. It was what I needed to get out of the doldrums; I was eager to shed the persona I seemed to have gotten mired in after too many personal sorrows.

At Publicis, I was offered the opportunity to lead Razorfish Health. Once a very large agency, Razorfish had diminished to a more modest size. My job was to reinvigorate it and build it back up. It was the first time that I knowingly took on a job where I was designated, from the start, as a change agent—and I took that to heart.

I let some of that former diplomacy I'd prided myself on as the Senator fall by the wayside. I wasn't at Razorfish to be a politician. I was there to pinpoint the good (and build on it) *and* to flag the bad (and change it). I was there to identify what was broken and come up with a plan to fix it, not to sugarcoat the truth. So that's what I did—but not at first.

My first day at the agency, I showed up in my best suit, highlighted the key talking points of my résumé as a form of introduction, and gave the team a big motivational speech about how we were going to turn this agency around! It was a very rah-rah cheerleader-style moment. About three weeks in, I realized my hyperpositive approach wasn't going to incite the overhaul that Razorfish needed. It was going to take some serious shaking up to achieve a meaningful transformation that would make a real difference.

So I brought about thirty-five senior functional leaders to an all-day off-site meeting. When they arrived, each one found two objects at their seat—a copy of a book called *Grit*, by Angela Duckworth, a professor of psychology at the University of Pennsylvania, and a compass. I then introduced myself to the team all over again—I mean *really* introduced myself—and I explained why I'd given each of them those two objects.

Introducing myself this second time, I skipped the shiny career highlights. Instead, I told the team about my grandfather, who escaped the Armenian Genocide in 1915. I told them about my father, an immigrant kid born in a row house in Watertown, Massachusetts, in 1921, and how, after high school, he got a job working at a gas station. He went on to fight in World War II, and he was in France on June 6, 1944. He earned a Purple Heart that day.

The point? Grit runs in my blood. According to Duckworth's theory, a person's success isn't about determinants like IQ, wealth, or family status. It's about your willingness to get knocked down, pick yourself up, and keep moving. We were going to need that kind of grit if we were going to reinvigorate Razorfish Health.

However, we couldn't move forward blindly. We needed to know where we were going. That's why I'd also given every person in the room a compass. We needed to define our own north point for the agency, to figure out the best path forward. There was a clear destination, but it was on us—as a group—to figure out how to get there. We spent the rest of the day in breakout sessions, having honest conversations about the agency, where it stood, where we wanted it to be, and how we were going to get there.

That meeting became the kick-start moment when I committed to enacting fundamental change at Razorfish—and when the people there joined me in that mission. From the time I started to the time I left, Razorfish more than tripled in size—in terms of staff, clients, offices, and revenue. What started as one location in Philadelphia grew to four offices, with additional offices in Chicago, London, and New York. That growth wasn't easy. We had to shift the agency's positioning, make management changes, find new clients, and reinvigorate old clients.

It was kind of like running through a burning building—you're hoping that you get out of the other side okay. But I wasn't afraid, because my hair had already been singed by all the change thrust upon me in my personal life. Plus, I wasn't in it alone. I had a team by my side every step of the way through the flames. But we had to have some tough conversations and hash out some harsh truths to emerge from the fire unscathed.

Change Needs a Vision Backed by a Clear Purpose: Finding Inspiration at Health Monitor

It was through my experience at Razorfish Health that I started to develop the playbook I use today to spur organizational transformation. I also began to appreciate the value of transformation more deeply. Done right, transformation benefits all involved. The ability to pivot and embrace new possibilities is beneficial for employees, customers, and stakeholders. Evolution is critical; without it, organizations run the very real risk of dying out—again, Kodak, Blackberry, Blockbuster Video.

That change-ready mindset accompanied me as I stepped into the role of CEO of Health Monitor in late 2020. By the time I came to the company, I had already embraced my role as a change agent. I had an approach I knew I could rely on to revolutionize an organization, transforming everything from a company's positioning to (most importantly) its people. The question was, Could I enact meaningful change at Health Monitor while still upholding the company's core values—and paying tribute to its long-standing reputation of excellence?

A forty-year-old media company, Health Monitor got its start creating "health condition guides" for patients so that they could better understand their diseases and treatment options—essentially spearheading so-called point-of-care media. Health Monitor's founder, Eric Jensen, had recognized that knowledge is power—nowhere more so than in healthcare. When patients get a diagnosis, they need information about the disease and its symptoms, progression, management, and treatment. Health Monitor's guides provided exactly that information.

When Health Monitor got its start, there was no internet. So to get that information to the people who needed it, printed guides were placed in physicians' offices, where patients could easily access them. While the company started to digitize in later years, it also stayed true to its print media roots. This proved challenging when the COVID-19 pandemic hit, and more patients were turning to telehealth or postponing in-office visits, in hopes of avoiding crowded waiting rooms.

When I joined Health Monitor, the company was grappling with the ripple effects of COVID-19 internally and externally. Within the company, people were adapting to work-from-home life. Beyond the company's walls, physician appointments were being postponed, and patients were increasingly experimenting with telemedicine. Recognizing these trends, many of the pharmaceutical companies and other healthcare stakeholders that had previously sponsored the distribution of some tens of millions of informational healthcare publications decided to press pause.

As a result, Health Monitor got disproportionally hit by the pandemic. There was an urgent need to pivot. We had to bring this historically print media business fully into the twenty-first century so that we could continue to do our small but meaningful part in communicating information to patients. Since then, we've taken what was a great company and made it even greater. We've modernized, embracing digital more fully. We've gotten rid of silos and improved transparency. We've adapted our business relationships, sustaining existing long-term relationships with pharmaceutical companies while also establishing new partnerships with *those* companies' advertising agencies.

In a short time, Health Monitor has become a more modern, agile, and successful organization—and it's because the company and its people were ready and willing to change. Further, that change was born of a shared commitment and a shared belief system.

Health Monitor isn't based on *my* values; it's based on *our* values as a company. We treat our customers a certain way. We treat each other a certain way. We always keep that end consumer, the patient, in mind. And I think that's made all the difference. What makes Health Monitor special is that it's a company with purpose. And that's what change requires—purpose. It also requires a leader who can help articulate and reiterate that purpose, an individual I like to call the storyteller-in-chief.

Change Requires Courage: Inspiring Change as a Storyteller-in-Chief

These stories from my time at P&G, Razorfish Health, and Health Monitor are only a small part of my journey. I've worked for many other companies (and held a variety of roles, from marketing to sales and leadership) throughout my career of thirty-plus years. Through all those experiences, I've learned some important lessons about what it takes to enact meaningful, lasting change at an organization. Health Monitor's evolution is a culmination of that journey, a model for organizational transformation that I hope can benefit others.

People would rather know they're building Notre-Dame Cathedral than just chiseling stone.

Ultimately, if I had to boil down what I've learned in my tenure to one thing, it's that change relies on people. For them to buy into transformation, to make it happen, you've got to give them a vision.

People would rather know they're building Notre-Dame Cathedral than just chiseling stone. Toward that end, you can't just develop a strategy for change. You need to have a story, and you have to evangelize that story with great persistence and consistency. That's why I sometimes refer to myself as a storyteller-in-chief.

You have to be able to tell people why the boat they're sailing isn't going in the right direction or is in danger in rough seas (and might even sink). Then you've got to help them prepare to come about—that moment when a skillful sailor changes the direction of their boat with one swift swing of the boom. Coming about is the only way to sail onward. But it requires everyone on the boat to understand the change that's about to happen. They have to know to watch their heads as the boom swings from one side to the other with great force. And they have to be prepared to not lose their footing. It's the most exciting—and maybe the most dangerous—moment on the journey.

When you look at it that way, it's no wonder we shy away from change. Change is scary. It's hard. There's a reason the treadmills at gyms are packed on January 1 and empty again by March 1. People inherently don't like change. We are creatures of habit. We get comfortable in our little routines and in our narratives about who we are and how our lives are supposed to go. But, as I well know from my own personal experience, change is also inevitable. So why not learn how to make the most of it? That's what this book is all about.

There Is No Rulebook for Change (and That's Not What This Book Is, Believe It or Not)

I mentioned some of the personal tragedies that helped transform me from a guy who was always playing by the rules to a guy who's more interested in challenging the rules. Like I said, I was not one to color outside the lines (again: Naval Academy!). Over time, my perspective shifted, thanks to my personal experiences as well as the experiences I gathered spearheading change at companies like Roche, Razorfish, and—more recently—Health Monitor.

Now I think of myself as a champion of change, not only for myself but also for others. We can all benefit from coloring outside the lines now and again. However, that involves giving up some level of control—a lesson that was hard for me to learn, if I'm honest.

My evolution as a father is a great example. One of my daughters was getting ready to graduate from college, and I fully anticipated she'd immediately start her own climb up the corporate ladder, much like I did. Imagine my surprise when she told me, "I think I'm going to take some time, go out West, and work on a dude ranch in Wyoming. I'll start my career journey after that." Part of me—the old Dave—wanted to say no. Old Dave would have told her to stick to the rules. Go to college, graduate, get a job with the "right" company, get a car, get a house—and so on.

But this was after my wife's death. New Dave was at the helm. So instead of trying to argue against my daughter's plan, I said, "Let's go get you some cowboy boots." She probably thought I'd lost my mind, but she appreciated my response. I didn't try to force her to play by my rule book. Instead, I let her write her own rule book.

That's what I hope to do with this book. It's not meant to be a prescriptive guide to how to achieve organizational change, because every organization is unique. Nobody knows your organization better than you do. I certainly don't. Instead, this book suggests some of the building blocks people can use to achieve meaningful transformation—like honest stocktaking, a shared vision, and a clear purpose informed by communal values.

People can change; I'm proof of that. Companies can change; Health Monitor is proof of that. Everything in life is about being able to make pivots. If you see an opportunity to take something good and make it even better, fear shouldn't stop you. I'm hoping that my own journey from rule player to change agent can help others (and help them avoid some of the mistakes I made along the way). Because, ultimately, we all benefit from positive change—and having not only the knowledge but also the confidence to evolve is something we all deserve.

PART 1

HEALTH MONITOR

CHAPTER 1

HEALTH MONITOR, THEN AND NOW

Health Monitor has long been a pioneer in the patient education business. It's a company of action, not inaction. The thing about pioneers is that they can't get complacent. If you're going to be among the first to implement a new concept, technology, or activity—the first to stake out new territory—you've got to keep pushing.

There's a need for constant introspection. You have to keep asking yourself, "What could I do better?" And you've got to have the grit and tenacity to answer that question honestly and (the tricky part) to then act on the answer. Health Monitor's transition from purely print to predominantly digital publishing is a testament to that fact.

When talking about transformation, what's interesting about Health Monitor is that—for more than thirty years of the company's history—it was exclusively a print magazine publisher. Up until about 2017, Health Monitor published some twenty million magazines a year on all kinds of medical topics, from lung cancer to diabetes, cardiovascular disease, and more.

Health Monitor was recognized as a long-standing, tenured, proven source of healthcare information. That information was distributed through physicians' offices—specifically, the waiting rooms. The company had built up relationships with more than two hundred thousand physician offices throughout the United States. Across the country, doctors were requesting these print publications to include in their waiting rooms, where patients could easily access them.

But, let's face it, print magazines alone are no longer the central element of a modern omnichannel media plan. So around 2017, Health Monitor started moving—gradually—into the digital space. By the time I joined the company in 2020, this digital transition had already begun. However, progress to becoming the market leader in digital was taking longer than desired. So it was on us, as a company, to figure out what we were doing wrong. We had to ask that tough question: *What could we do better?* And stomaching the answer wasn't easy at first.

Transformation Begins on the Inside: The Day I Threw My Desk Phone in the Trash

When I joined Health Monitor in late 2020, I was given a clear objective: help the company continue its pivot to a modern digital platform. So you'd think I'd start by sitting down with our content team, riffing on ways to adapt our print content for our customers in order to meet twenty-first-century digital needs. But, to me, that wasn't the right place to begin. I knew that this transformation would have to start *internally*. We had to look inward before we could adapt outward.

When I walked into my office on day one, I saw I had a desk phone—a clunky landline telephone, complete with all the "modern" gimmicks, like speakerphone and the ability to switch between multiple lines. Again, this was 2020. The first thing I did on that day? I unplugged that monstrosity and threw it in the trash. I'll be honest with you—I still don't have a dedicated in-office phone. If somebody needs to get ahold of me, they can reach me on my mobile phone. They can call it twenty-four hours a day, seven days a week. Who needs a desk phone?

That move prompted me to look at Health Monitor's in-house technology. We had a gentleman named William Saint-Louis on staff. Will had an incredibly in-depth background in information technology platforms, gained at some very large technology companies. But, since Health Monitor remained predominantly (by definition) a legacy print publisher, Will hadn't (yet) been given the chance to flex his strategic IT muscles. He was running a tiny internal IT department that was mostly dealing with mundane issues, like connecting desk phones and resolving daily tech problems.

Will was an incredible untapped resource—a wealth of IT knowledge—who had been underutilized. We had to give him free rein and personal agency to help bring Health Monitor's internal IT operations into the twenty-first century. Since then, the IT department has more than tripled in size—and Will is at the helm, as executive vice president, chief technology and digital operations officer. His job description was completely reframed. Flash-forward to today, and he's no longer servicing desk phones. He's helping to develop the next generation of Health Monitor's digital screens, complete with 5G—slicker, faster, and better than ever.

Will's story is a clear example of a case in which we had marvelous talent within the organization—but we weren't fully utilizing it. If you have a Ferrari, you don't want to leave it sitting in your garage. I don't want to suggest that I'm comparing human beings to cars. But the point is this: if you've got a spectacular car, you want to take it out on the open road and see what it can do. If you've got spectacular people, you want to give them some freedom and see what they can accomplish.

If you have a Ferrari, you don't want to leave it sitting in your garage.

Change starts with people. And Health Monitor has an outstanding history of employing outstanding people. But if we aren't leveraging those people and their talents optimally, what's the point? To be a pioneering company, we need pioneering people. Our Health Monitor change story begins and ends with people—people like Will.

Investing in the Right Technology: The Birth Control Lesson

While we were revamping Health Monitor's internal processes—the IT department being just one point of change—we were also looking at how to bring Health Monitor's business model as a whole into the twenty-first century. Take one of the company's most significant products, the patient education guide, as an example. These guides facilitate conversations between doctors and patients, giving patients the information they need to better understand disease symptoms, management, and treatment options.

When Health Monitor was founded, those patient guides were print publications. Now we have digital patient guides. How did we make the jump? I can clearly pinpoint the transitional moment when we stepped firmly from the past into the twenty-first-century digital future. It was the needs of college-aged women that inspired us to do better.

Early on in my tenure at Health Monitor, my sales team and I were sitting in front of an agency that was talking to us about a client that was launching a birth control product. The target audience was young women who might be getting their first birth control—often from on-campus health centers. How could we appropriately educate those young women about their options? The obvious answer was the same one we'd always had: give them a patient guide. Put that printed patient guide in the waiting rooms of on-campus health centers, where they'd have easy access.

But I had raised two daughters who, just recently, had been in college. I knew that these girls were not going to walk across the quad, from the campus health center to the dorm room, with a printed brochure about birth control sticking out from between their stack of books. They just weren't going to do it.

Then we realized: college girls like my own daughters might not grab a brochure. *But* they might download a mobile app for more information.

They might not take the time to read through the patient information leaflets of various birth control products. *But* they might take the time to complete a BuzzFeed-style interactive quiz to help determine which method of birth control was right for them.

They might not read a medical paper by a Harvard Medical School ob-gyn to better understand potential birth control options. *But* they might watch a video featuring that same leading ob-gyn, boiling down the same essential information—methodology, safety, contraindications—into an easy-to-digest short video clip.

So that's what we proposed. Within seventy-two hours, we took the concept of the traditional printed patient education guide and transformed it into something sleeker and more modern—something that actually met the needs of the target audience in question. Trying to give college-aged girls in the twenty-first century information about birth control via print materials was like trying to win a race against Henry Ford's automobile while driving a horse-drawn carriage. We saw that we had to make our own car to keep up.

That one project—a birth control information campaign—was pivotal. We saw, very clearly, how embracing new technologies would help us continue our long-standing mission of educating patients. We weren't going to get rid of print completely—and we don't plan to, as we believe that print media still has its place in the patient education pipeline. By maintaining digital *and* print products, we can foster inclusivity and give all patients a medium that meets their needs (something I'll discuss more in the next chapter).

Still, by harnessing the power of digital, we were able to leverage a new way to speak to patients. And it was something we could get excited about. We weren't just creating a digital pdf version of a print guide. It was a completely reimagined experience, including videos, quizzes, and interactive content. That high level of innovation is what we wanted to carry forward.

Bringing Patient Communication into the Physician's Exam Room: A Pioneering Step

The birth control lesson was valuable. It showed us what was feasible. With its unique target audience—young women born in 2000 or later—the case exemplified the need to embrace digital more fully. It also helped crystallize the possibilities. Apps, quizzes, videos, interactive content—these were things that print didn't allow for. With digital? We had a world of opportunities, of various ways to reach patients and resonate with them, at our fingertips.

Inspired, we ramped up our investment in digital screens. But we weren't just striving to change the media format. We were also making a strategic bet on the location of those screens. Instead of digital screens in the waiting room like so many of our competitors, we saw that the real power lies in the *exam* room.

The decision to implement digital screens in the exam room predates my time at Health Monitor. That savvy business move was made in 2016 by Eric Jensen, Health Monitor's original founder and CEO. Eric was the guy who said, "Hey, we're going to launch this new platform of digital screens. And we're going to put them in the exam room, not the waiting room." So the original concept addressed not only the media format—a digital screen—but also the placement of that media. And that was a very important decision.

The exam room, where a patient and physician meet, is a sort of sacrosanct space.

To me, a digital screen carries a different psychological weight when it's in the exam room, not the waiting room. When people are in the waiting room, they're flipping through their *People* magazine or scrolling on their phone. Once their name is called, and they've taken those ten steps to the doctor's office, they're no longer interested in celebrity gossip. Now they're ready to have a real conversation—a serious one. They want to know what's going on with their health—arguably any individual's most valuable asset. They're going to be attentive, asking questions and seeking information.

On top of that, the exam room, where a patient and physician meet, is a sort of sacrosanct space. It's understood that what's said there is confidential, in line with the Health Insurance Portability and Accountability Act (HIPAA) privacy laws. People tell their doctors things they might not tell their dearest friends or even their family members. And the exam room is where it happens. You're not going to get into the details of your condition or your symptoms in the waiting room, in front of a bunch of strangers. It's all happening behind that closed door.

The exam room is also a special place because it's *only* for the doctor and the patient. Pharmaceutical sales representatives aren't entering the exam room. They can talk to the doctor in their office or in the lobby—or in a hallway or the break room. But they can't go into the exam room. That protected space is for the doctor and the patient alone.

Shifting the screens from the waiting room to the exam room elevates the message. The patient is now receiving information in a sacrosanct, protected space—the exam room. That brings a different psychology with it, adding a weight and a seriousness to the interactions and informational transactions that occur in that space. In short, people feel that they can trust what they learn in an exam room.

We place innate belief in our healthcare professionals—and that carries over to the information we receive in the healthcare spaces where we interact with those professionals. For example, 85 percent of Americans rate nurses as having high levels of honesty and ethics.[1] And 68 percent of adults value information received in the doctor's office.[2] By providing information at the point of care, Health Monitor

---

1   R. J. Reinhart, "Nurses Continue to Rate Highest in Honesty, Ethics," Gallup, January 6, 2020, https://news.gallup.com/poll/274673/nurses-continue-rate-highest-hon-esty-ethics.aspx.

2   Hensley Evans and Victoria Summers, "The Evolution of Point-of-Care Marketing in Pharma," ZS Associates, 2017, https://pocmarketing.org/wp-content/uploads/2022/01/Evolution-of-Point-of-Care-Marketing-in-Pharma-ZS-study.pdf.

can better reach patients in a way that serves them—while they're still there, in that sacred exam room, able to ask their doctors questions (and get answers they trust).

Investing in the Right People: The COVID-19 Lesson

As Health Monitor started to step more confidently into the digital space, we got plenty of confirmation that we were making the right move. Not only were we reaching more patients but also our transition toward digital was proving to be business savvy. As we pivoted from a dominant print focus, our most recently launched digital products quickly came to represent almost 10 percent of Health Monitor's revenue (which was, as a whole, growing). We could see that we were on the right path. We weren't yet where we wanted to be, but we were optimistic.

Health Monitor has always been—and still is—in the patient education business. But let's get real: the money to create informational materials like the traditional patient education guides has to come from somewhere. So Health Monitor materials also include branded messaging, developed in partnership with pharmaceutical and medical device companies. That's where the commercial side of the business comes into play. As a marketing partner, we're able to secure the funds we need to get those patient education materials made.

So when COVID-19 hit, and patients were, temporarily, no longer filling up waiting rooms, Health Monitor faced a challenge. Some people were staying home, pushing off nonurgent medical appointments, to avoid infection. Others were bypassing the doctor's office completely, turning to telemedicine for help. Even when patients were still going to the doctor, they were often no longer in a physical waiting room. Instead, they were in their cars in the parking lot, waiting to be called in individually from outside. The car was the new waiting room, temporarily.

Brands and their agencies were, understandably, rethinking the role of materials that were meant to sit in waiting rooms now that those waiting rooms were often ghost towns. Contracts were paused. Tough discussions were had. Everybody had to pivot. It was, to say the least, a chaotic and challenging time—not only for Health Monitor but also for people all over the world.

In Health Monitor's case, there was a silver lining: we had already created the transition from the waiting room to the physician's exam room. And that sacrosanct space was where we could still reach patients. Going ahead, that's where we had to focus our energy and resources.

As with our IT transformation, this also required some internal changes—and, of course, it required people to make it happen. In short, it meant a cultural overhaul. We were proud of the new tech we had developed. The question now was, How were we going to get our digital screens into *more* physician exam rooms—and how were we going to demonstrate their value to our marketing partners, the ones who were essentially paying for those screens?

It meant revamping two core components of Health Monitor's business. First, we had to build up our boots-on-the-ground team that advocates for our physician network. These are the men and women going out and engaging with physicians' offices every day, all across the country, letting them know about the free educational products we provide—at no cost to them—and asking if they want to join our physician network. That team had been cut down in the years prior to my joining Health Monitor. We decided it was time to build it up again.

So we brought in some fresh blood and hired Robert Dougherty, a professional with a strong pharmaceutical industry sales leadership background. We told him what our objective was—and then we trusted him to meet that objective, leaving the expansion of that physician office network in his and his teams' capable hands. And that's exactly what he did. Under Rob's guidance, we got more people pounding the pavement and meeting with doctors. Now our physician office network has a larger footprint than ever before.

We also had to reconfigure our sales team's approach to our customers—pharmaceutical companies and their advertising and marketing agencies. We had to revisit old relationships and build new ones—and, again, we needed the right people to make it happen. This time, we didn't have to look far to find the perfect fit.

We had an internal individual who was fantastic at managing accounts, Augie Caruso, whom we promoted to a key account management role. And, as with Rob, we then stepped back and let Augie have free rein—and he delivered. He's now our executive vice president, key accounts. We also brought in an external sales professional, Keith Sedlak, who had a pedigree of managing sales organizations in marketing services. Keith brought some fresh perspectives that further helped elevate our sales team. Now? He's our executive vice president, chief growth officer.

These are just a small handful of the people who helped steer Health Monitor safely through the storm of COVID-19. There are many others, more than I could name (I'd have to write a whole other book) who played their part. Weathering this period of rapid change required everyone to really dig in and work hard—and work hard *together*. The Health Monitor team managed, transforming how we engage with patients, physicians, and customers. And it all started with investing in the right technologies—and the right people.

Investing in the Right Communication Strategy: The Transparency Lesson

Getting people on board with change means communicating about it. You can't implement some cloak-and-dagger approach and turn a company around overnight, secretly, without *telling* people about it (or, if that's possible, I'm not aware of it). This is another point where Health Monitor offers a compelling example. To make the changes I described earlier, we had to embrace transparency, opening up communication in a way that the company hadn't previously.

Again, we had to start on the inside. This time, I wasn't tossing an old desk phone in the trash. I was overhauling the way that people within the company, at all levels, communicated and interacted with one another. It required getting rid of some hierarchies. It required reducing silos. And it required, above all, buy-in from Health Monitor's people. I couldn't just talk the talk and *say* we were going to remove hierarchies and silos. I had to walk the walk.

When I joined Health Monitor in 2020, we were in the midst of the COVID-19 pandemic. The entire staff was working remotely. Only a handful of people from the senior team were still coming into the office (hey, I had important on-site business to take care of, like trashing desk phones!). It was an eerie sight, pulling into a parking lot that holds three hundred cars and seeing only five or six vehicles in it. It felt like a ghost town—even more so when I made it to my quiet office.

I realized that if I wanted to change the direction of the company, I needed to communicate with people. And me sitting alone in an office (and them sitting at home) wasn't going to work. So I started doing monthly CEO videos to open the lines of communication. I would literally sit on the edge of my desk in a pair of jeans and a sports coat and riff off a five-minute video that got distributed to all the employees. And that video laid bare the facts.

Our employees wanted to know what was going on. Especially in the nerve-racking uncertainty of the pandemic, people were craving honesty and certainty. Those videos were our chance to provide that transparency. I was telling them, "Hey, we've made some organizational changes. Here's why. Hey, we just finished a quarter. Let me tell you about the financial results. Hey, we're investing more money in digital screens. Here's the reason for that."

It was the first time that people had seen that level of transparency—about organizational change, about financial numbers, about company investments. The feedback from our employees was overwhelmingly positive. Those five-minute videos became must-see TV because they had information that actually mattered to our employees. Later, we took it a step further and opened up the floor to *them*, creating a two-way communication channel with the occasional live Zoom town hall. This gave everyone, whatever their position, a chance to speak up and ask questions.

That commitment to transparent communication was critical at the time, not only because we were making major organizational changes but also because of the distance imposed by the pandemic. It wasn't just a question of the content we included in those CEO videos. It was also a question of the format. Video was more personal than a long-winded email (which, let's face it, probably would have been skimmed, at best—or, more likely, immediately moved to the junk folder).

Video also gave all those remotely working employees a chance to actually *see* me, this new guy who had stepped in as CEO in the midst of a pandemic (they must have thought I was nuts). Finally, through video, I could better shift the tone of how we were running the company.

Before I'd joined Health Monitor, the office was fairly formal—think business clothes and executive washrooms. Now the new CEO was sending out videos of himself wearing jeans, sitting on the edge of his desk. It helped set the tone. People who had been with the company when it was still a place where jeans were forbidden could see me and think to themselves, "Well, if the CEO's going to sit on the edge of his desk in a pair of jeans, I guess jeans aren't forbidden anymore."

Something small and seemingly superficial like that (I mean, yeah, it's just a pair of jeans, right?) spoke to the bigger changes afoot. We wanted to give people permission to take initiative. I didn't want to be a tightly regulated, hyperstrict, top-down organization. We wanted to empower our people to take smart, logical action—and to work together. And that required getting rid of some of those symbols of hierarchy and rigid structure—like a constricting suit and tie—and embracing transparency.

As we brought that transparency to our internal operations, we also started to push it externally. Historically, Health Monitor had closely guarded information about its industry-leading physician office network—how many doctors we worked with, where, in what specialties, and so on. Even though we had this large footprint of physician network offices with an industry-leading reach, we weren't sharing the granular data about that network with the ad and media agencies that were working for our clients (pharmaceutical and medical device companies).

Some agencies had been asking for that data for some time—understandably, since it would allow them to better plan their clients' media initiatives. So when I stepped in, I decided it was time to let them look behind Oz's curtain. I called up some key agencies and told them, "Hey, I know that you've been asking to look at our network. Let's see what we can do." So we put in place the appropriate legal partnering language to protect our databases—for example, we added terms restricting data sharing—and then we let them see the data.

We knew that these agencies could better plan for their clients— also our clients—if they knew details like what physicians' offices in our network worked in cardiology, dermatology, or gynecology, for example. So we handed over those lists. That unprecedented openness got results—results for our clients, who could plan their media budgets with greater transparency and confidence, and results for our business.

These are just a couple of examples of how Health Monitor has lived up to its promise of greater transparency, both internally and externally. And we've all reaped the rewards. But it all started with something as simple as those little CEO videos. If you want to change the direction of a company, it's a lot like coming about, swiftly swinging the boom to change the direction of a sailboat. Those videos were our first step in coming about—swinging the boom.

Transformation Doesn't Mean Changing *Everything*: Maintaining Quality Content throughout Health Monitor's Evolution

As a legacy print publisher, Health Monitor was acknowledged by many as the gold standard for the creation and distribution of patient education print titles. This wasn't just a question of having a far-reaching footprint, spanning some two-hundred-thousand-plus doctors' offices across the country. It was also a question of the quality of content.

This is something that I personally place a premium on. I believe it is our purpose as a company to provide accurate, validated, comprehensible information that patients *get* in a language they understand and in a format they are comfortable with. And I believe that purpose is important—and that it can't be just a job. It has to be a passion. From my personal experience, I know all too well how important it is for patients to have access to the right information at the right time.

When my mom was sick and dying with cancer, I remember my father being overcome with emotion. The grief that that kind of earth-shattering diagnosis brings is profound. I also remember how bewildered he was. He basically needed a translator in the room when my mom had her medical appointments, because the information surrounding her diagnosis was so dense and complex. Especially back then, resources were less readily available. You needed somebody to help make sense of that complex medical jargon, to untangle all those big polysyllabic Latin words.

Having witnessed and experienced that need for facts firsthand, I have a deep appreciation for Health Monitor's mission to provide quality, accurate information to patients. We don't just hang TV monitors up in doctors' offices, slap a brand logo on a video, and walk out the door. That's because we aren't a media placement company. We are, first and foremost, a health education content company.

We have an in-house editorial and content team of heavily cre-dentialed health journalists crafting our content in partnership with a bespoke group of medical advisors. Our Medical Advisory Board includes key opinion leaders (KOLs) across a diversity of specialties, from cardiovascular health, to neurology, obstetrics and gynecology, and more. These KOLs—hailing from some of the best educational institutions in the country, like Harvard Medical School, Johns Hopkins, and Yale—are openly identified on the Health Monitor website. Together with our in-house editorial and content team, they help ensure that Health Monitor's content is credible and trustworthy and that it has a value-add for patients.

We also have a number of alliance partners, like the American Academy of Cardiology and the American Heart Association, who review content. In some cases, they'll add their own imprint to that content, giving it their expert stamp of approval. That's another signal of credibility, another verifiable testament to the value of Health Monitor's educational materials. At a glance, a patient can see, "Hey, this information was reviewed by this doctor from Johns Hopkins and by the American Heart Association," and they can feel confident that the information they're getting is solid.

Whether we're creating print or digital content, these KOLs and alliance partners are a critical part of the process—and they have been for decades. We have always taken these relationships very seriously, because healthcare information is a serious topic. Yes, Health Monitor is a commercial enterprise that helps to build brands. But at the end of the day, we're helping patients gain access to health information, and we have to make sure that information is honest, relevant, and credible.

We also want to make sure that others in the point-of-care space are held to the same standards. That's one reason Health Monitor helped found the Point of Care Marketing Association (POCMA) in 2013. According to POCMA, "point of care" is defined as the moment a patient gets care through an interaction with a healthcare professional in a healthcare setting. This could include not only doctors' offices but also hospitals, pharmacies, nursing facilities, and even virtual care. Point-of-care media—like the screens Health Monitor has in physician exam rooms—aim to facilitate discussions between patients and healthcare providers in these spaces.

POCMA exists to uphold a commitment to honest, reliable information for *all* point-of-care information and marketing providers, not just Health Monitor. That said, I'm proud to say that Health Monitor's print *and* digital footprint has been audited, validated, and certified by POCMA.

We've also gotten external validation elsewhere. For example, Health Monitor has consistently won National Health Information Awards, which honor the nation's best consumer health programs and materials. In 2018, Health Monitor got bronze. In 2019? Bronze. In 2020? Gold, silver, *and* bronze. In 2021, gold, silver, and bronze *again*. We've been upping our game, and the accolades reflect that. Of course, we aren't in it for awards—but hey, some external recognition never hurt, right?

The Final Piece of Health Monitor's Transformation Equation: Change Rooted in Shared Values

We've established that change is tough—but also that it's possible. To me, the Health Monitor story is a prime example of this truth. This is a company that's been around for some forty years. The business has always centered around one purpose: creating educational materials to facilitate the conversation between the patient and the physician.

But the content and the way it's presented—from printed magazines in the waiting room to screens in the physician's room—has evolved. And while we still absolutely have print products—for reasons I'll explain in the next chapter—those print products have been reformatted and upgraded (for example, all print products now come with digital companion products). So at the end of the day, Health Monitor is now a digital-first company, not a print-first company.

I've summarized five years of intensive change for Health Monitor, both internally and externally, in about four thousand words. And I'm painting a pretty rosy picture. That might make the process sound easy. It wasn't. It still isn't. But Health Monitor has a clear vision of what it is and what it isn't, and that clarity of vision has helped guide the entire journey. Health Monitor never strived to be like the ad agency plastering a billboard in Times Square. We're building content, not placing ads. We see ourselves as a medical education company, and that role brings great responsibility with it.

Healthcare is, without exaggeration, a life-or-death field. Through our small but important role as an information provider in that field, we want to make sure we're doing right by the real heroes—the patients and

> **Health Monitor never strived to be like the ad agency plastering a billboard in Times Square. We're building content, not placing ads.**

the physicians who treat them. I know my role. I never wake up in the morning thinking that the Nobel committee is going to come knocking on my door to give me the Peace Prize. But I also know that if the information we provide helps spur the conversation between the physician and the patient, helps the patient understand the mechanism of their disease or their treatment, then we've helped, in our own small way.

That's something I'm incredibly proud of. And it's an ethos that I think the people at Health Monitor share. That pride informs our employees' dedication to the company—and our company's dedication to taking care of our employees. I'm truly gratified to say that Health Monitor has been certified as a Great Place to Work for 2019, 2020, 2021, and 2022—and hopefully beyond. Being able to maintain that credential even in the tough COVID-19 years, throughout the transitions described earlier, is a testament to Health Monitor's successful cultural shift and its ongoing adherence to the core values of transparency, initiative, and teamwork.

The only people who can truly, honestly judge whether we're adhering to those values are the people who work here. That's why getting that Great Place to Work certification is such a big deal to me. Yes, I've talked about some other awards we've won or certifications we've received—and I've mentioned some other metrics about our growing network and increasing profits. But revenue isn't the right metric all the time.

Ninety percent of Health Monitor's employees say they have faith in management and would recommend working at Health Monitor. That's a more genuine marker of success, in my view, than raw numbers alone—especially when talking about transformation. And that transformation journey of Health Monitor's isn't over. I certainly hope the sailing is a little smoother ahead, now that we've set the course and the boat is on the right path. But we'll always be ready to pivot. Because, as we've learned, it's not only necessary—it's also how we elevate our company and ourselves.

That ability to pivot remains essential, because Health Monitor's transformation isn't complete. In this chapter, I've talked about changes we've already made and suggested how similar initiatives, like greater transparency, might benefit your organization. Looking ahead, the future of Health Monitor promises even more evolution. And there are plenty of lessons there for you too—something I get into next.

CHAPTER 2

THE FUTURE OF HEALTH MONITOR

Following a period of rapid transformation, it's tempting to sit back and relax. We were certainly tempted to hit pause and take a breath as Health Monitor's evolution took hold. We had upgraded our technology. We had restructured some key departments. We had adapted our communication processes, internally and externally. And we had ensured that we had the most up-to-date bespoke content, all while making a continued commitment to quality information.

It was *a lot*. For everybody involved. Not just me. So, understandably, everybody was ready for a breather. But Health Monitor is, at its heart, a pioneering company, one devoted to action, not inaction. So we didn't stop. Today, Health Monitor continues to keep a pioneer spirit alive by constantly exploring how to improve our offering in a way that benefits our partners—as well as the patients and physicians we ultimately strive to serve.

Throughout my various roles as a change agent—or storyteller-in-chief, as I like to call it—I've learned that change is a constant process. This holds especially true for a company like Health Monitor, which operates in healthcare, a field that's constantly evolving. Personally, I think that evolution is for the better.

> **Throughout my various roles as a change agent—or storyteller-in-chief, as I like to call it—I've learned that change is a constant process.**

The growing attention given to health disparities and the call for greater health equity is one compelling example of how healthcare is coming to better serve more patients' needs. The question is, How are we at Health Monitor going to contribute to that conversation going ahead?

This is just one of the tough questions we are asking ourselves in our continual change process. We've also got to ask if we're keeping up content-wise, staying abreast of the latest medical breakthroughs in treatment areas. We've also got to ask if we're keeping up tech-wise, making the most of cutting-edge innovations to enhance our media platform. And, as we ask those tough questions, we've got to commit to fully exploring the answers and continuing our change journey in the future.

Transformation truly is a never-ending story. One look at Health Monitor's current work and future plans makes that clear.

Adapting to the New Healthcare Landscape

Change isn't just a constant process. It's also a process affected by all sorts of external factors. It doesn't happen in a silo. Health Monitor's experiences in health equity is an excellent example. Over the past decade, experts have raised the alarm about health inequities in the US. Racial and ethnic health disparities in the US have very real consequences, including higher rates of certain chronic disease among minorities. Take diabetes, for example: the prevalence of diagnosed type 2 diabetes among non-Hispanic whites in the US is 7.6 percent, compared to 12.8 percent among Hispanics and 13.2 percent among African Americans.[3] And that's just one disease category.[4]

So, at Health Monitor, we have to reflect on our role in this equation. What can we do on our side, as purveyors of health information, to make a change? We refuse to think that diversity and health equity are just a matter of changing the photo of a cover subject from an African American to an Asian American person or from a Caucasian person to a LatinX person. It is fundamentally and foundationally about building the right content to meet the needs of all patient groups.

Yes, we are a digital technology platform company. But, at our heart, we remain a content company. So we've realized that we need to stay abreast with the most-up-to-date content. Of course, we want to include the most current clinical content, sourced from verifiable, scientifically backed medical journals. This ensures that we are giving patients the most salient facts. However, we also want to ensure that we're creating content that serves all patients, not just a subsection of the population.

We have a valuable platform. We're in the room, giving physicians and patients direct access to educational materials. How do we

---

3   J. E. Rodríguez and K. M. Campbell, "Racial and Ethnic Disparities in Prevalence and Care of Patients with Type 2 Diabetes," *Clinical Diabetes* 35, no. 1 (2017): 66–70, http://doi.org/10.2337/cd15-0048.

4   "The State of Health Disparities in the United States," in *Communities in Action: Pathways to Health Equity*, eds. A. Baciu, Y. Negussie, A. Geller, et al. (Washington, DC: National Academies Press, 2017), https://www.ncbi.nlm.nih.gov/books/NBK425844.

leverage that platform in the interests of health equity? Again, as we started exploring this question, we had to look internally to find our starting point. One thing we've done is to evolve our Medical Advisory Board. We've expanded our panel of advisors, adding more diverse voices from experts who can help pinpoint gaps in our content.

As one example, we've added Julius M. Wilder, MD, PhD, to help accelerate our health equity work. He's an assistant professor of medicine at Duke University; the chair of their medical school's Diversity, Equity, Inclusion, and Anti-Racism Committee; and the vice chair of the Duke Department of Medicine's Minority Retention and Recruitment Committee. In addition to Dr. Wilder, we've got Leslie S. Eldeiry, MD, FACE, of Harvard Medical School, who also focuses on diversity, equity, and inclusion topics. We're continually looking to expand and diversify, inviting more voices to the table, so that we can ensure all patients' needs are represented and improve the content, making it most relevant for a specific patient audience.

This kind of approach has become ingrained at Health Monitor. Just like when we revamped our IT or our sales departments, we are creating change by implementing the right people. We are finding experts who know their stuff in both medicine and the health equity space and bringing them on board. That kind of expertise benefits us as a company and benefits the patients and physicians we serve. We've added these folks because we know that health equity is critical to making sure that patients— all patients—get the information they need to understand their disease and embark on their treatment plan.

Keeping Up with Content: Identifying and Overcoming New Hurdles

The previous example shows one of the many ways that Health Monitor is continuing to update its content. While embracing larger industry changes, we've also got to maintain that commitment to quality that we've adhered to throughout Health Monitor's transformation journey. This is what lets us occupy that sacred space I spoke about in the first chapter—the physician's exam room. I firmly believe that it's our commitment to quality content that allowed us to enter that space, and that's something we can't lose.

With our screens, we tell an educational story about a disease state, the symptomology, and the way a treatment might work. We strive to answer the kinds of questions a patient might want to ask their doctor. Yes, we also subsequently deliver an advertising message. However, the primary aim is to give the patient the language and information they need to confidently engage in a conversation with their doctor.

We've come to realize that this work is more critical than ever—and that it faces more challenges than ever. Why? Health misinformation is running rampant. Modern tools that enhance everyday convenience, like mobile phones and social media, are changing the way we communicate about fluffy things like pop culture (share your thoughts on *Hamilton* on Twitter!) and food (post the pic of that dish on Instagram!)—as well as serious things like politics and, of course, healthcare.

The COVID-19 pandemic was a great example. Faced with a novel viral mutation with unprecedented impact (both on individual patients and on health systems), the world was scrambling for information. We were in uncharted waters, all of us. Unfortunately, this opened the floodgates for speculation and misinformation to enter the conversation. The World Health Organization (WHO) even has a term for it—*infodemic*, which refers to the dissemination of "false or misleading information in digital and physical environments during a disease outbreak." According to WHO, "It causes confusion and risk-taking behaviors that can harm health. It also leads to mistrust in health authorities and undermines the public health response."[5]

Even beyond COVID-19, health misinformation is of increasing concern. A 2021 study found that health misinformation on social media covers an array of topics, from vaccines to drugs, smoking, eating disorders, noncommunicable diseases, and medical treatments—including treatments for cancer.[6] That's scary stuff, in my world. The thought that people are getting information—*wrong* information—about cancer treatments from social media is sobering.

So, again, as with the health equity situation, we at Health Monitor have to ask ourselves—what can *we* do? With our tiny bit of power, our small presence in the physician's exam room, what's our role in this?

Fist, we can continue what we're already doing: maintaining a commitment to scientifically backed, verifiable, quality content. We still have our in-house editorial and content team of health journalists, led by our long-term editor-in-chief and senior vice president of content, Maria Lissandrello. Her team is augmented by our Medical Advisory Board of KOLs. Above all, we continue to think of ourselves

5   Anna Harvey, "Combatting Health Misinformation and Disinformation: Building an Evidence Base," Health Affairs Forefront, November 23, 2021, https://www.healthaffairs.org/do/10.1377/forefront.20211118.932213.

6   Victor Suarez-Lledo and Javier Alvarez-Galvez, "Prevalence of Health Misinformation on Social Media: Systematic Review," *Journal of Medical Internet Research* 23, no. 1 (2021), http://doi.org/10.2196/17187.

as a content-first company. Yes, of course we have branded sponsorships from pharmaceutical and medical device companies that want to deliver an ad. But we build our content first. And that's the priority.

We've also expanded our visible partnerships with well-known patient organizations and advocacy groups—recognizable brand names that patients recognize and therefore know they can believe in. Names like the American Lung Association or the American Cancer Society are familiar and trusted. Other partners range from the American Association of Clinical Endocrinology to the National Headache Foundation and the Coalition of State Rheumatology Organizations. If we've got content about it, we try to find a trusted partner to back that content.

Our partnerships with these advocacy groups add another level of gravitas to our content—a verifiable stamp of approval, attesting to the quality and correctness of the information. These alliance partners review Health Monitor's content independently, ensuring it meets their stringent criteria, before allowing their brand to appear on it.

It's another component in our checks-and-balances system. We have our in-house expert healthcare journalists creating the content. Then we have a relevant KOL from our Medical Advisory Board review it. And, finally, we've got a fully independent third-party organization giving it the nod of approval as well.

We believe that having the relevant industry group additionally review that content ensures that what we're creating is not only accurate but also fair, unbiased, and in the patient's best interests. We've also found that physicians really embrace this approach. Having those big names on the content that appears in their offices adds legitimacy. It also reassures the patient, presenting them with a name they recognize, even if they aren't a medical expert themselves. In my view, that's a value-add that benefits all involved.

Our Commitment to Upholding Health Monitor's Point-of-Care Marketing Association Certification

Our POCMA certification is another example of how inviting external parties into the content conversation can help elevate that content, benefitting all involved. POCMA puts forth rigorous auditing and verification standards to help hold the point-of-care industry accountable, checking that content is accurate and ensuring that honest business practices are upheld. Health Monitor's entire print network already carried the POCMA seal before the company transitioned more fully to the digital realm. In early 2022, we were also able to get our *entire* digital screen network platform POCMA certified.

This is something we aim to uphold going forward. That POCMA seal is a testament to the quality and reliability of our data. It can help reassure physicians and patients who use our content. It can also help reassure a client who is buying media from us; they can proceed with total confidence, knowing that an independent third party has audited our content. A prospective buyer at a media agency can be certain they're getting content that's validated, verified, and independently checked by an objective body.

While our POCMA certification is valuable to us at Health Monitor, it also provides value to the other players in the field—like the companies investing in our products and, most importantly, the healthcare providers and patients who use our products to facilitate discussions. You can't just *tell* people you're trustworthy (well, you can try, but it probably won't get you far). You've got to *demonstrate* that you're trustworthy. Show, don't tell. Prove it. Our POCMA certification lets us do just that. By holding ourselves to this high standard, we promote transparency and trustworthiness. It's also the right thing to do from an ethical standpoint—a mindset that is part of our core values at Health Monitor (and something I'll speak on further in chapter 6).

Maintaining Technological Relevance: Continuing Self-Assessment to See What Works (and What Doesn't)

Looking into my Health Monitor crystal ball, there's the evolving content aspect to consider in the future—factoring in changes like ensuring greater inclusivity while still maintaining existing content standards. But there's also the technology aspect to consider.

We were the first in our industry to market innovations like in-flight campaign measurement and healthcare practitioner omnichannel engagement platforms, inclusive of healthcare practitioner social engagement. That's a legacy we want to uphold with our future technology. But the tech world is evolving at a breakneck pace, a fact we're very cognizant of. Those shiny new screens that look so flashy and modern right now? They may not look so impressive ten, five, or even three years from now. So we've got to do our research. We've got to keep up.

Logically, when you're implementing change, you're hoping it's going to have a positive impact. That means you've got to take the time to step back and see what your changes are accomplishing (or failing to accomplish). Health Monitor today is a great example of this, thanks largely to the data we're able to collect from our screens and their primary users—physicians.

What does a patient see when they're in the physician's exam room with a Health Monitor screen in front of them? As I write this, those screens consist of panels that rotate automatically every twenty-five seconds. The idea is that a patient is often passive while in the physician's room. You might be sitting there in that awkward paper gown, partially dressed, so getting up from the exam table to go swipe a screen for more info doesn't make a lot of sense. By keeping info on the screen active, we're making it easier and more comfortable for the patient. You can jump off the table and swipe to move the information along—but you don't *have* to.

Although our screens are programmed to move through panels independently, they also offer the option to swipe ahead. The patient or physician can move information along on the screen by swiping across it with their finger. We've found that this flexibility is something physicians really embrace, largely due to the nature of our content.

Our screens include content rich with detailed, fact-checked medical information. So one panel might include an in-depth anatomical drawing of a lung, and the next panel might include a detailed animated video showing how the lungs function in action. A doctor who's trying to explain to a patient how the lung works and how the patient's lifestyle choices—say, smoking—are impacting the lungs, might swipe to those screens to help make their point clear.

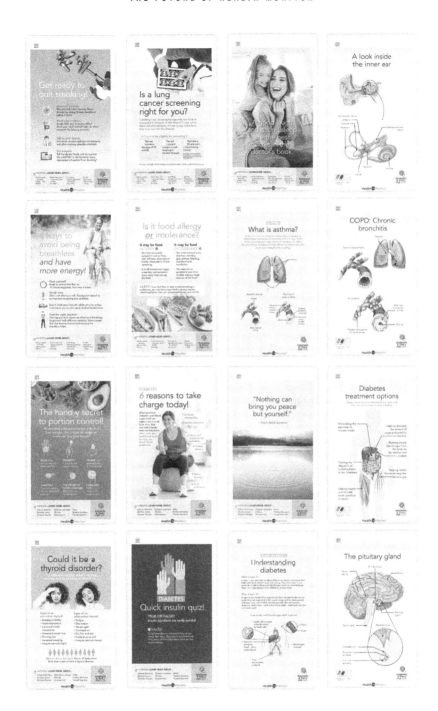

Examples of real-life Health Monitor digital screens.

When we made our screens touch-friendly and built in that swipe option to move the content along, we didn't know for sure that physicians would make use of that possibility. So we went back to the doctors and asked them. And, based on our survey, we've found that approximately 90 percent of physicians who have Health Monitor screens in their exam rooms will, at some point during their workday, make use of the swipe function. They'll go over to that screen and say to the patient, "Hey, let me show you what I'm talking about." And then they'll zip through the navigation menu so that they can say, "Here's how the kidneys work" (or whatever the topic may be). Based on the feedback we've received, we're confident that the swipe functionality has a value-add for doctors and patients.

Now that's just a qualitative survey of physicians we've worked with. For the future, Health Monitor is determining how to further leverage our digital screens for data collection in a way that benefits all stakeholders involved. Our next-generation digital screens are even sleeker and more elegant—and they encompass 5G technology, improving functionality and reliability. They also make it easier to capture data.

Ideally, we want to be able to take quantitative data about how our screens are used and bring that back to advertisers so that they can concretely see the real-time return on investment, or ROI, they're getting. So if we've got the physician using a screen as a digital teaching tool, clicking on drop-down menus to visit certain panels—say, a diagram of how the heart pumps blood through the body—we can track the clicks, swipes, and time spent. How often does that one info panel get pulled up? How much time is spent on it? With more granular metrics like these, we can really focus on what's useful to physicians and patients—and we can show our advertisers demonstrable ROI.

Imagine if we have data like that coming in from fifty thousand or sixty thousand screens—or more—across the country. That gives us a great ultra-quantitative metric of the value these digital screens hold as a teaching tool in a patient consultation. That kind of forward-looking vision encapsulates all the things that make Health Monitor unique. You've got quality content backed by verifiable experts; screens placed in doctors' exam rooms instead of waiting rooms; and cutting-edge technology that's user-friendly—and, in the future, going to provide even more valuable metrics.

Those three things coming together is what I think gives Health Monitor a competitive edge. That trifecta is what makes the product unique and special. However, I also know we'll have to continue putting ourselves and our products under the microscope if we're going to maintain that competitiveness. We've got to consider what works and what doesn't. And, sometimes, as I discuss in the next section, what works best isn't necessarily the most cutting-edge technology—but a simple printed magazine.

Why We're Keeping Our Print Products (and Making Them Better)

Health Monitor's future is bright. It's modern. It's digital. Over the last two chapters, I've explained how Health Monitor transformed from a legacy print-first to a digital-first company. I've told you all about our shiny new screens and the stats we gather from them. And I've told you about how we're upgrading our content, striving to make it better, more inclusive, and more encompassing. But now I'm going to let you in on a secret: after all that effort (and financial investment!) in making those changes, in bringing Health Monitor to the twenty-first-century digital age, we're still creating print products.

Yep.

Wait, don't close the book yet. We really *aren't* some stone-age company, clinging to the vestiges of what some might view as an old-fashioned media format. I promise!

Yes, we've concentrated great time and energy on shifting to digital. The company made a major capital expense commitment building out its network of digital screens. And, as I mentioned in the previous section, we're going to continue to push forward in terms of innovation—for example, by enhancing our screens with 5G functionality.

But we are also maintaining our long-standing leadership presence in print publishing. Why? Because we recognize a very real need for it. Contrary to what some people say, print is not dead. And we think that print products still have a very important place in the market.

Part of this is an accessibility question. Often, the people who are dealing with the tough diagnoses are older individuals, those who may not be as tech savvy as younger generations. At the time when my father was grappling with my mother's diagnosis, he certainly wasn't running to Google to look up information.

On that note, we have to consider that many of the people who use our patient guides are seniors. Many diseases, from cardiovascular disease to diabetes, gain prevalence with age. So when we talk about serving patients, that frequently means people sixty and up. And people in that age bracket tend to engage with information, especially digital information, differently. Why wouldn't they? A twenty-year-old who was basically born with a smartphone in hand is certainly going to absorb and process information differently from an eighty-year-old who spent the bulk of their life in a world where smartphones didn't even exist.

There's data to back this up. For example, a national survey regarding readiness for digital health strategies in the context of COVID-19 examined whether people were ready to use health apps for tasks like contact tracing. The elderly were among those who were less likely to be open to this kind of technology.[7] So if older patients are hesitant to use apps, we don't want to give them an app solution for acquiring valuable health data—we'll save that medium for college-aged women.

Another study reveals that while older adults are willing to look up health information online, they lack the confidence to assess the quality of the information they find.[8] That's where having a recognizable, trustworthy organization's stamp of approval can help. So that's why we seek collaboration opportunities with organizations like the American Lung Association and the American Cancer Society.

And it's not just seniors. Beyond those sixty and over, there are still plenty of people out there who are more comfortable with print than digital media. And think about simple access. There may be people who don't have the technology readily available to access all our digital products. Or there may be people who simply prefer print.

So recognizing those accessibility needs and the wants of all patients, Health Monitor doesn't have a plan to put away print com-

---

7   V. Sounderajah, J. Clarke, S. Yalamanchili, et al., "A National Survey Assessing Public Readiness for Digital Health Strategies against COVID-19 within the United Kingdom," *Scientific Reports* no. 11 (2021), https://www.nature.com/articles/s41598-021-85514-w.

8   A. M. Turner, K. P. Osterhage, J. O. Taylor, A. L. Hartzler, and G. Demiris, "A Closer Look at Health Information Seeking by Older Adults and Involved Family and Friends: Design Considerations for Health Information Technologies," *American Medical Informatics Association Annual Symposium 2018* (December 2018): 1036–45, https://www.ncbi.nlm.nih.gov/pmc/articles/PMC6371280.

pletely. We think print still has a very important place in the healthcare information system.

We also want to think about how people absorb information. Some research suggests that people actually comprehend information better when they read it in print instead of digital formats.[9] There have also been studies suggesting that people understand information better if they're taking notes.[10] This is something that's made easier with printed materials.

A person can grab a magazine, take their pen, and scribble away. They can underline the words they don't get and want to look up. They can highlight points they want to ask their doctor about. And they can mark passages they want to show a loved one. In some cases, bringing home a simple magazine from the doctor's office that clearly explains the intended treatment plan is a lot simpler and more straightforward than directing someone to a website or an app.

So Health Monitor's decision to keep print products isn't a question of maintaining some kind of historical print legacy arm for ego purposes. And it's certainly not a decision made from the bottom-line perspective. It's about catering to consumers' needs and wants and promoting accessibility to health information on all fronts. Again, this is part of the Health Monitor commitment to being a content-first company. We want to give people information about health topics in a way that's relevant, timely, and accurate—and that is compatible with their needs. And that means *all* patients' needs.

---

9   Pablo Delgado, Cristina Vargas, Rakefet Ackerman, and Ladislao Salmerón, "Don't Throw Away Your Printed Books: A Meta-Analysis on the Effects of Reading Media on Reading Comprehension," *Educational Research Review* 25 (2018): 23–28, https://doi.org/10.1016/j.edurev.2018.09.003.

10   Mark Bohay, Daniel P. Blakely, Andrea K. Tamplin, and Gabriel A. Radvansky, "Note Taking, Review, Memory, and Comprehension," *The American Journal of Psychology* 124, no. 1 (2011), 63–73, https://doi.org/10.5406/amerjpsyc.124.1.0063.

When my late wife was diagnosed with lung cancer, I spent many hours with her in the waiting rooms of oncologists and lung specialists. Lung cancer is a very complex diagnosis. There are loads of questions. What are metastases? Why are we doing a gene-type testing? What is EGFR (epidermal growth factor receptor)? How is that different from ALK (anaplastic lymphoma kinase)?

The point is: it's complicated. It's confusing. It's foreign. And, to top it all off, it's scary. When I think about the other people I saw in those waiting rooms at the time, most of them were older people, some old enough that they may not have been comfortable with the latest tech. The last thing we want to do as a company is to make a diagnosis like lung cancer even more overwhelming—for example, by asking our audience to download an app when they rarely use apps. So if Health Monitor, by continuing to offer print patient guides, can help make things a little less complicated, confusing, foreign, or scary for such patients and their loved ones, I consider that a success story. I consider that something worth maintaining.

That's not to say our print guides haven't changed. Today's printed patient guides look very different from five years ago or even one year ago. We've strongly branded them with the Health Monitor Living brand name so that people know they're getting information from a trusted source. We've modernized and contemporized the visuals and the content. And the print products have a companion digital product that patients can access via a QR code on the printed guide.

Of course, we've also made sure that all that new information is reviewed by a KOL from our Medical Advisory Board and by a third-party patient or physician advocacy group. So the content is still of the highest quality, but it's being delivered and packaged in a way that is right for the time and for the person in question.

When it comes to sharing information about birth control for college-aged women, an app makes the most sense. When it comes to sharing information about a disease like Alzheimer's or age-related macular degeneration, is an app the best conduit of information? Maybe not. Maybe a printed guide is better. I think we will retain things like the printed patient guide because they matter for certain people at certain times. And I think it's about retaining the most salient information in the appropriate format and for the right reason— because you're putting the needs of the patient, not the business, first. That's something Health Monitor wants to maintain as it continues its change journey.

Health Monitor's Change Journey Isn't Complete (and Neither Is Mine ... and Odds Are, Neither Is Yours)

It would be incredibly arrogant for me to present the Health Monitor story as being *finished*—because it isn't. Far from it. I would love to offer you a clear, linear narrative that ends with a bright and shiny package—the new and improved Health Monitor! But that's not the reality. The reality is that we continue to change and are committed to continuing to change—always in service of getting better.

I think Health Monitor is a great lesson of the value of accepting that infinite nature of transformation. It's a lesson that can be hard to stomach at first. I know firsthand, because it took me a while to swallow that pill. I mean, you put all this effort into a transformation and then you want to sit back and enjoy the effects. Your change project—be it a personal or a business endeavor—emerges from its cocoon, and you want to watch it soar off like a beautiful butterfly. Your job is done! If only this were the truth.

Transformation requires ongoing effort. And people who really commit to change, who commit to being change agents, know that they need to keep asking the tough questions. How can we do better? It's like the gym analogy: you can't go to the gym for six months and then stop cold turkey and expect all those gains you worked so hard for to hold up. If you quit now, you might backslide and end up right back where you started.

> **Transformation requires ongoing effort.**

Of course, you might not have to grind as hard as you did at first. The initial impetus for making a change does require the most effort—the most blood, sweat, and (sometimes literal) tears. It *does* require less energy to maintain after that first spurt of metamorphosis—the grub crawling out of the cocoon and spreading its wings into a butterfly. But it still requires time and attention. You've got to nurture that butterfly if it's going to maintain and go places. You've also got to consider the surrounding environment and how *that's* changing.

Health Monitor's journey speaks to all those points. Yes, we took this fantastic legacy print media company and transformed it into a digital-first media platform. But that process isn't finished. We're still asking ourselves the tough questions, considering how we can change to

- keep up with the evolving healthcare landscape (taking into account needs like health equity);

- maintain high-quality content (especially in the face of healthcare disinformation); and

- ensure our technology remains at the forefront (by continually revisiting our tech and gathering feedback on its usage).

Only by addressing all three of those points are we able to, in good conscience, stay in the room. I've reiterated (maybe more times than you'd like to hear) how much value we place on the fact that we're permitted to set our digital screens not only in the waiting room but also in the physician's exam room, that sacred space where doctors and patients have the real conversations (sometimes tough conversations). If we're going to keep that space in the room, we have to remain flexible. And we have to continue challenging ourselves.

The end of the story isn't really written. That holds true for my own personal transformation. It also holds true for Health Monitor's transformation. And it holds true for whatever transformation journey you are currently on or considering embarking on (or thought you had concluded—hate to break it to you, but it's probably not over yet). And the sooner we can all accept that, the more change-ready and capable we'll be. That knowledge will also help us accept that discomfort that change often, inevitably, brings with it—a discomfort that is ultimately for the better.

Embracing Discomfort Going Ahead—Because That's Where the Best Changes Can Happen

It might seem disheartening at first. Here I am, telling you, "Change is never ending—you'll be hacking away at it until the day you die!" Again, the gym example is a good one. Investing in your own health— for example, with regular physical activity—is a lifelong process. You can't put in a few good years of eating right and hitting the gym and then transition to sitting on the couch and chowing down on burgers every day—not if you're trying to achieve good health outcomes. The same is true if you want good *change* outcomes.

As I've said, the journey isn't always comfortable. In Health Monitor's case, the COVID-19 pandemic certainly led to some very uncomfortable growing pains. But all that discomfort turned out for the best. While I like to be a provocateur, I certainly would never say COVID-19 was a good thing. It wasn't. It was a terrible global pandemic that impacted lives and businesses and economies and families.

But, much like in my own life, in Health Monitor's case, the hardship made us better. I don't wish hardships on anybody, personally or professionally. But they're inevitable. They're going to come. So the question is, How are those hardships going to make us better?

For Health Monitor, I think that COVID-19 made us a more digital company. It meant that our field organization that calls on physician offices had to get comfortable working in a remote environment—because they couldn't see physicians in person. It meant that we had to ramp up our digital screen presence in physicians' exam rooms—because the waiting rooms were often, temporarily, empty. It meant that we had to reconsider our relationships with advertisers—who didn't want to invest in print products for waiting rooms when those waiting rooms were deserted. Finally, it helped assure us that the future was digital, and it convinced us to focus our efforts and our capital expenditures in that direction.

Again, I can't take credit for a lot of that. In fact, I can't take credit for *most* of it. Health Monitor founder Eric Jensen was the person smart enough to say, "Hey, we're not going to just offer print products; we're going to use digital screens. And we're not going to just put them in the waiting room; we're going to put them in the exam room." The seeds of the great idea had already been planted.

However, it took some pressure from COVID-19 to convince us to water those seeds more vigorously, to ensure that they would grow.

Finally, the hurricane that was COVID-19 meant that we had to be more attentive and conscientious than ever before to the quality and veracity of the content we produced. The infodemic surrounding COVID-19 was a tough reminder of the significance of accurate, verifiable health information. We became even more aware of the importance of ensuring that we weren't contributing to healthcare misinformation—not just in relation to COVID-19 but in any area.

COVID-19 also helped drive home—not only for Health Monitor but also for the healthcare sphere at large—the importance of combatting health disparities moving ahead. I touched on this topic at the start of the chapter, explaining how Health Monitor is seeking to do our small part to improve health equity. And, again, I hate to credit the black-hatted villain of the play, COVID-19, with anything *good*—but there is a silver lining to the fact that COVID-19 helped unmask the harsh reality of health disparities in our society.

According to data from the Centers for Disease Control and Prevention (CDC), Black or African American people were 2.9 times more likely than non-Hispanic white people to be hospitalized and 1.9 times more likely to die from COVID-19 infection. Meanwhile, Hispanic and Latino people were 3.1 times more likely than non-Hispanic white people to be hospitalized and 2.3 times more likely to die from COVID-19 infection. American Indian and Alaskan Native people were 3.7 times more likely than non-Hispanic white people to be hospitalized and 2.4 times more likely to die from COVID-19 infection.[11]

---

11 Centers for Disease Control and Prevention, "The Unequal Toll of the COVID-19 Pandemic," March 12, 2021, https://www.cdc.gov/coronavirus/2019-ncov/covid-data/covidview/past-reports/03122021.html.

Experts have theorized many reasons for these disparities, including the prevalence of preexisting medical conditions, like type 2 diabetes, in certain communities. Other possible factors range from location to healthcare access and flat-out racism.[12] Health disparities aren't a new thing. COVID-19 just helped highlight a preexisting problem—and it really drove home the fact that these health inequalities exist, take a real toll on people's lives, and need to be addressed.

Of course, these aren't problems for Health Monitor alone to solve. But, as I said, we felt a responsibility to do our small part. As servants in the healthcare system, providing information for physicians and patients, we have a responsibility to look at the big picture and consider what role we can play to help—for example, by ensuring an inclusive approach when we create our content and considering the needs of all patients, not just certain subsets of patients. So, also in that sense, COVID-19 was the tough, uncomfortable reminder we needed, staring us in the face to do better. We want to remain open to discomfort and even lean into it, knowing it will get us to a better place.

What's Next for Health Monitor (Spoiler Alert: I Don't Know for Sure)

I've been very candid about the ups and downs of the Health Monitor transformation journey. So now you might be wondering—was it all worth it? Yes.

---

12   Daniel C. DeSimone, "COVID-19 Infections by Race: What's Behind the Health Disparities?" Mayo Clinic, April 2022, https://www.mayoclinic.org/diseases-conditions/coronavirus/expert-answers/coronavirus-infection-by-race/faq-20488802.

When you do good work, when you improve for the better, other people notice. This is a fact I can attest to not only through my experience at Health Monitor but also throughout my career as a change agent. We were thrilled when Health Monitor's transformation started getting positive attention, not just among our immediate clients but more broadly.

Health Monitor's content has consistently earned recognition. We've repeatedly won Hermes awards, for example. Hermes is one of the oldest and largest creative competitions in the world, with winners ranging from individuals to media conglomerates and Fortune 500 companies. Health Monitor has been recognized since 2018, and in 2022 we won platinum and gold for newly relaunched creative and content. Health Monitor has also been recognized for excellence in marketing and communications with multiple MarCom Awards (platinum and gold in 2018, 2019, 2020, and 2021).

Of course, as already mentioned, the recognition I'm personally proudest of is the Great Place to Work certification, because it testifies to the fact that, throughout the Health Monitor transformation journey (and the chaos of COVID-19), the company didn't forget what matters most—the people who hold it up. Those are the people who made the change possible in the first place. Where would we be without them?

When I look at Health Monitor, I still see plenty of changes ahead. But I'm also very excited for those changes. There's a technology chapter that's certainly still being written. But there's also a content evolution that's taking place and making us into a more modern, progressive twenty-first-century organization.

I've already addressed some plans for the future—like improving our commitment to inclusive healthcare content and gathering user data from 5G-enabled touchscreens. We're also looking beyond these more immediate steps. We're exploring telehealth. We're researching remote patient monitoring applications. Finally, we're considering other delivery vehicles for content and thinking about other media formats, beyond screens, that we might use in the future.

I think that the breadth of our offerings will only continue to increase—not because we want to introduce the flavor of the month but because we want to continue to bring relevant innovations to patients and physicians.

But if you ask me what Health Monitor will look like in five, ten, or twenty years, the honest answer is that I can't tell you. That's because the transformation process is so multifaceted. It doesn't come from one person at the top. It comes from many people. And many internal and external forces influence that change process. COVID-19 is the prime example. I doubt many business owners had "global pandemic" written into their emergency plan of what-if scenarios. All of this might sound daunting. But it's also exciting. I'm looking forward to seeing where the world goes and what we need to do to keep being a value-added resource for patients.

The promise of future change is tantalizing—if you've got the tools to make the most of it.

The promise of future change is tantalizing—if you've got the tools to make the most of it. In the next chapters, I want to talk a bit about those building blocks for change and how to leverage them—so that you can get just as excited about change as I am. So that it doesn't feel like the unending slog of "Ugh, more change?" and instead feels more like a future full of promising possibilities.

That promise is what motivates the pioneer spirit. And that's the spirit that has allowed Health Monitor to pivot time and again. We pioneered point-of-care marketing in the healthcare space all the way back in 1983. We were a pioneer as one of the founding members of POCMA in 2013. And we were pioneers when we put digital screens in the physician exam room in 2016. Finally, it's that spirit of openness and adaptability that allowed us to shift from a legacy print publisher to a digital-first media company.

So I can't tell you exactly what lies in Health Monitor's future. But I can assure you of one thing—we'll be keeping that pioneering spirit alive. Next, I want to look at the building blocks you can use to embrace your own pioneering spirit. In my experience, it starts with the three Cs: culture, communication, and competitive advantage.

PART 2

THE THREE Cs OF THE TRANSFORMATION PROCESS

CHAPTER 3

CULTURE

I've been fortunate to lead transformations—sometimes called a restructuring or rebuilding—several times in my career. First at Roche, where I led the transformation of the US Diagnostics sales structure go-to-market approach, then at Publicis Groupe to restore growth to the Razorfish Health agency, and finally at Health Monitor. And there are, in fact, some common themes that run through all those experiences. What I have captured here is my three Cs approach.

I'm not about to lay out a fourteen-point plan or even a seven-point plan for you to follow. Because guess what? Transformation isn't that complicated. Ultimately, it comes down to three core components, what I like to call the three Cs: culture, communication, and competitive advantage. That simple idea works for whatever sector you may be in, whether it's pharmaceuticals, consumer package goods, or something else altogether. Maybe you sell knitted hats on Etsy. Whatever you do, the three Cs can help you implement change.

So let's start with the first (and most important, in my view) building block: culture. Culture is critical for transformation. It sets the stage for all action, the expectations of an organization, and the values the company will pursue. Culture must be addressed before any other aspect of a transformation.

Of course, leadership can set the tone for transformation, but it's only going to work if change is adopted more widely, at every level of the organization. *That* is when you get those great transitions, those incredible pivots that can turn around a failing company or take a great company and make it even better.

Culture must be addressed before any other aspect of a transformation.

If you check out a lot of those old business books, from the 1980s and 1990s (you know, the "classics" that many a CEO still has sitting on a dusty bookshelf in their office, whether they've read them or not), you'll find they tend to relegate culture to the back seat. They'll focus on points like changing out people and innovating products and turning around customer relationships. If these books talk about company culture and its role in transformation at all (most don't), it's usually as a brief mention toward the end. They'll rarely give culture (an admittedly difficult to define concept) a front row seat in the transformation conversation.

On the one hand, I get it. Culture is a tough metric. It's hard to measure, and in some cases, it's hard to determine exactly what smaller cultural changes will achieve the desired larger cultural shift. But the longer I stay in the business world, the more convinced I become of the importance of a strong, agile company culture, especially when it comes to achieving change in an organization. So that's why I decided to put culture in the spotlight for this chapter.

Transformation requires transforming company culture. And not just transforming it in a superficial way—for instance, by instituting new policies—but transforming it in both thought and action, at every level, both internally and externally. In my various roles, I've found that the transformation process I use when engaging with a company (*any* kind of company, from media agencies to consumer goods producers and beyond) requires a high-level shift in culture and, with it, leadership. The starting point? Defining the right values.

The Significance of a Parking Space

When I arrived at Health Monitor, on my very first day as CEO, I felt that the cultural piece was the most important thing to do—and to do with both speed and care. The first step? Defining the values that would guide our transition. So I put the proverbial flag in the ground, marking three values that I thought were critical for the company's continued success: transparency, initiative, and teamwork.

Then I started looking at ways to crystallize those values. Basically, I had to show my team that I wasn't just *saying* we were going to value transparency, initiative, and teamwork. I had to prove to them that we were *actually* going to enact those values, concretely, throughout the company. I had to demonstrate that I, as a leader, was going to adhere to those values. Only then could I reasonably expect those around me to uphold those values as well. Fair enough, right?

Where to start? In my case, it began with a parking space. When I got to the Health Monitor corporate headquarters on my first day, I noticed that there were reserved parking spaces in front of the building. Those numbered spots—one, two, three, four, etc.—were reserved for the CEO, the CFO, and so on. I felt that if we were going to create a culture built on values like transparency and teamwork, that kind of hierarchical parking plan didn't feel right.

So I pulled the building facilities manager aside and told him, "I'd like you to paint over the reserved signs and the numbers in the parking lot so that they just become regular parking spaces that are available to anyone."

I remember he stared at me with this puzzled look on his face and said, "Dave, there's only about a dozen of you coming to the office right now. From a senior management perspective, what's the point?"

Remember, this was at the height of the COVID-19 pandemic, so most of the employees were working remotely, aside from a few senior executives. That massive parking lot was mostly empty at the time. It was a ghost town. But I told him, "Trust me, it's the right thing to do."

Culturally, I felt that small change—painting over some numbers in a parking lot—was a step in the right direction. It was going to get us closer to where we needed to be. And it would show people that we weren't just going to shout out those new values (transparency, initiative, teamwork). We weren't just going to trot them out in meetings or slap them onto our corporate brand Bible. We were actually going to live them. If I was the last one to show up at work on a Monday, I'd be the one who would have to traverse across the lot. If I was the first one to show up, I could park in that coveted front row spot.

So we made the change. And even though some 95 percent of the company was working remotely at that point, news about that little parking space paint job traveled *fast*. People heard about it and told others, and awareness of that small update went through the organization pretty quickly. I mean, I didn't enact this change for an intended effect. I enacted it because it seemed like the right thing to do. But people learned of it, and it immediately telegraphed to them that things had changed, *really* changed, starting on day one.

Identifying Cultural Components in Need of Change: Common Issues Companies Face

So the question is, What cultural components could change in *your* company? I don't know. Only you can determine whether your organization is living up to its cultural values. Maybe your organization doesn't have clearly defined values (or maybe they're outdated). In that case, the first step is to define those core cultural components that matter to your company and the people in it. You've got to plant that flag marking your values as the first step.

Exactly what those values *are* is up to you. But there are a few key components that I've tended to witness, repeatedly, throughout my various roles as a change agent in my career. Here are some common mistakes I've seen, again and again. By establishing fitting values in your organization, I hope you can avoid these errors yourself.

Siloed Business Operations

Siloed business practices are one problem I've seen seriously interfere with business success. Departments making decisions without considering how those decisions impact other departments can lead to chaos (not to mention plenty of friction between departments). So ensuring that people and departments are working together effectively is, in my view, a must.

That could mean changing internal communication protocols, for example, or adopting new internal communication tools (e.g., ditching old-school email for a more user-friendly and transparent project management system). Each organization needs to determine how it will break down silos and improve teamwork. And, odds are, your organization has some silos that need to be addressed (if you aren't seeing them, ask your team—they'll probably tell you).

The fact is that over the course of my career running agencies, big and small, one of the things I've consistently come across is that internal siloed thinking. In an agency, it could be between the creative department versus the strategy department versus the account management department, for instance. In a media company, it could be between the sales department versus the technology department versus the content department. It depends on the structure.

One way to address those siloes is to ensure, from the get-go, that you have a well-functioning, trusting, and collaborative senior leadership team. Logically, you can't eliminate all those individual departments and just mash everything together. So you've got to have strong leaders in each one who are able to bridge the gaps.

Usually, one of the first things that has to happen in a transformation initiative is that you must get your senior leadership team sitting at one table. And you need to include *all* departments, not just the "biggest" or the "most important" ones. Every department needs to have a seat at the table. Everyone needs to have a voice. Everyone needs to see the information.

This also means actively recognizing the value of all departments and reiterating that regularly. Every team has a function and a skill. If you aren't including every department, you are implicitly questioning their craft and their value to the company. When you're having a big budget meeting that impacts the whole company, don't just include accounting and HR and sales. Include your art director. Include your content director. Include your facilities manager. Whatever your organizational structure may be, include your senior leadership team from *all* departments.

I get that these are different crafts and that the content of some meetings may be more relevant to one department than another. But the walls of those functions need to be permeable membranes, such that information flows freely and is shared and that one department is not more or less important than another.

Cocktail Napkin Deals

Siloed business practices often go hand-in-hand with secrecy and side deals, or what I like to call cocktail napkin deals. You know the kind: two colleagues go to lunch outside of the office, chat about a project, and come to an agreement—sketched out on a cocktail napkin—without following the proper protocols or including all relevant parties in the conversation.

This goes in direct opposition to core concepts I personally ascribe to and have implemented in my transformation efforts: transparency and equality. Or, as the French would say, égalité—that concept of equality (social or political) first voiced in 1789, during the French Revolution.

Strong culture tends to stem from a feeling of togetherness. Hierarchical structures counteract this (one reason I decided to paint over those parking lot numbers). If you want to say, "Hey, we're in this together," you've got to show that you're an organization that deals with people in a transparent and fair manner. Nowhere is this more apparent than in a company's reward structure (or lack of structure).

Disparate reward structures are again something that I have seen many, many times in my career. A company will have two people in the same role in the same department, but they have disparate financial rewards. And this tends to go hand in hand with those cocktail napkin deals. People will say, "Here's the official policy, but here's the deal we can do on the side" (for example, to bump up a person's base pay with a bonus that not everybody gets).

In an ideal world of égalité, there should be no side deals. I know, I know: we aren't living in an ideal world! Nonetheless, this is a major red flag that I've always acted against quickly, and I strongly suggest other business leaders do the same. It's a topic that can easily be brought up in an initial round table with that senior leadership team and something that's best addressed swiftly.

In my past transformation experiences, I've gotten all the senior leadership team into a room early on and I've told them, "We're going to make the reward mechanisms and bonus structures consistent and transparent. If you're at the director level, you know what your compensation can be. If you're at the vice president level, you know what it can be. And you can be confident that each person in your similar level is being treated in the same way."

People respond to that positively. Nobody wants to run the risk that they're going to be the one left out or left behind in terms of pay. Certainly, nobody wants to learn that their work is worth less than their colleague's, especially if they're doing the exact same job at the same performance level. The calls for greater transparency around pay in recent years (and workers banding together to proactively share their pay via online platforms) is a testament to this fact.[13]

---

13   Michelle Fox, "Are You Being Paid Fairly? Young Workers Share Salary Information as Pay Transparency Gains Steam," CNBC, April 27, 2022, https://www.cnbc.com/2022/04/27/young-workers-share-salary-information-as-pay-transparency-gains-steam.html.

Policies protecting pay equality and transparency are increasingly in demand. Such policies are sound business decisions. And let's face it: such policies are simply the right thing to do.

A Lack of Transparency

Siloed business practices and side deals share a common foundation: a lack of transparency. This is another problem I've seen many companies run into. I've already spoken about some of the ways I tried to improve transparency at Health Monitor. I briefly mentioned the CEO videos I started making when I stepped into my role— for example, sharing information about the company openly with employees (including data they hadn't been privy to in the past, like financial numbers, clients we'd won or lost, and so on).

As we were kicking off those videos, our chief communications officer asked me, "Do we need to make these videos password protected so that our employees can't share them? What if they get out beyond the company? What if our competitors see them?"

I thought about it, briefly, and then told them, "Just put the videos out there using our standard file-sharing link. No password needed."

I decided that if the culture was supposed to be about transparency, then that meant we should be able to trust one another. And, frankly, if someone wanted to share one of those videos, it wasn't a problem. I was an open book. Those videos were simply telling the story of our company, a story I was happy to shout from the tallest mountaintop (and still am—hey, I'm writing a whole book about it). So why bother with secrecy?

Nonetheless, it was an interesting moment, one where we had to grapple with the old-school mode of thought, the kind of culture that would have embraced numbered parking spaces and password-protected company videos. The thing is, we had already decided to move beyond that kind of culture. This was yet another opportunity to demonstrate our commitment to that change.

Transparency can also be lived out in simple process changes. For example, say you get all your department heads in the room for one meeting. Whether it's in person or via Zoom or whatever, you want to make sure everybody has their say and that everybody gets it all out *in that meeting*. I'm not a huge fan of the meeting after the meeting, as I like to call it. In my experience, it plays out something like this: we've had a productive meeting, we've all disbanded, and then someone who didn't say much during the actual meeting approaches me with a just-one-last-thought kind of comment or question.

When that happens, I make a point of shutting it down right away. At the end of a ten-person meeting, we've presumably articulated some agreement or decision. As a leader, it's on me to make sure we live out that agreement or decision in a transparent manner, in a way that respects all ten people who were in the room when it was made. If the meeting is adjourned and someone then tries to talk to me about what's just been decided, that doesn't seem fair. I tell them, "I'm really sorry. That got adjudicated in front of everyone. It's not fair to those who aren't here now to have this conversation a second time. Unless you want to bring all ten people back into the room, I'm not having this conversation with you."

It only takes a few moments like that, where you call a time-out and say, "We're not going to readjudicate this. It's done," for people to learn that you mean it. And then you stop getting pulled aside for the meeting after the meeting. I'm all for debate and for dissenting opinions. That's usually how some of the best work gets done. If everyone's just saying yes to everything in a meeting, you've got a problem on your hands. However, I want dissenting voices and debates to take place when all relevant parties are present.

Side conversations tend to muddy the waters. They also reduce transparency. Finally, they hurt trust. If I were to engage in a side conversation with one person in my ten-person leadership team, make a decision based on that conversation, and *then* revert back to the other nine people on my team—those other nine might feel (understandably) slighted. At best, they might feel that their voices weren't heard or that their opinions didn't matter. At worst, they might suspect favoritism.

A small step like eliminating the meeting after the meeting improves transparency and builds trust. It lets people know that there aren't side deals or side pockets of information and that there aren't some people with greater access to the CEO than others. Unfortunately, I've seen it the other way around so many times—and I can tell you, in most of those cases, it doesn't end well.

All-Around Negativity

This one is a little tricker, for a few reasons. First of all, *negativity* is a pretty broad concept. It's easier to identify than to explain. But we all know those companies—the ones where people schlump into work, late and unsmiling. The ones where everyday business meetings are heavy with tension. The ones where people work against each other, not together. The worst employee is the one who quits (emotionally) but stays.

On the flip side, we can all recognize a culture of positivity. I've had the privilege to work with many companies that really glow with a positive culture. These are companies where people are smiling. They're chatting at the coffee machine. They're supporting one another, cheering each other on. Where colleagues honor commitments to one another with work and deadlines because they would never want to let a colleague down. These are the kinds of companies we all want to work for. I'm lucky to have worked for many such organizations in my career, and I hope that you've had the good fortune to work for some too.

Another reason this is such a tricky point is that, if a company culture is pervasively negative, combatting that can be very tough. Negativity is, unfortunately, contagious. A bad attitude can trickle down from a manager to an employee, to another employee, and (in the worst-case scenario) to customers. What can you do to counteract it?

One thing I've found that works is simply focusing on the positives. For example, you might try implementing an on-the-spot bonus recognition program, something I've seen really make a difference. It's something we tried out at Health Monitor. If a member of the senior leadership team saw someone doing something good, excelling in some way, they had the authority to award them a bonus of X dollars on the spot. The leadership team had full authority. They decided who, when, and where to issue these bonuses.

As we rolled it out, I told them, "Let's catch your people doing something right." And that became the mantra of the program. So often, leadership focuses on catching things going wrong. If you're a parent, you know that it's way easier to catch your kid doing something they shouldn't (like sticking their finger in the light socket) than it is to catch them doing something they should (like making their bed without being asked).

Now I'm not comparing employees to children. But the point is that our society is broadly conditioned to fixate on what's going *wrong*, not what's going *right*. It's understandable; it's a defense mechanism, part of how we protect ourselves. This holds especially true for leaders, who often have to take the fall if something goes wrong. As leaders, we're always attuned to fixate on an error or what could become an error—the next fire that needs putting out.

I thought, "What if we turn it around? Let's start focusing on moments that are worthy of rewards rather than on moments requiring correction." So we rolled out this program of on-the-spot bonuses. Senior leadership didn't have to write a memo or get my sign-off on anything. They just went to HR and said, "Cut a check to Jane Doe on this date, because yesterday I saw her do this special thing." And that was it.

The initiative allowed for immediate recognition of those things that were consistent with our values. And I think that really helped reinforce some of those core values we'd set while also helping us maintain that sense of urgency and speed that transformation requires (something I'll go into more detail on in the next chapter).

The program wasn't just about recognition. It also *empowered* senior leadership and their people. If we wanted to achieve change quickly, we needed to move quickly, and that meant getting people to take initiative. An on-the-spot bonus scheme that highlighted the positives was one way to encourage people to take action without worrying that they'd get their hand slapped for trying something new. It helped create that culture of action, not inaction, that we wanted.

Implementing Cultural Change Practically: People, Processes, and Products

With these anecdotes, I'm trying to elucidate that muddy concept of culture, to show that it's not just an *idea*. I want to show how culture can be lived out and embodied in a company's practices and policies, concretely and tangibly. Again, I'm convinced that culture really is where all great change starts (and I'm determined to prove it to you).

Toward that end, I want to talk about the way culture can influence some core business components: people, processes, and products. First, let's admit that transformation means different things for different companies (and people). No two change journeys are identical. That said, most business transformations require a shift in at least one, if not all, of three core areas—people, processes, and products.

Most business transformations require a shift in at least one, if not all, of three core areas— people, processes, and products.

Those are some major components of a business, so changing them is no small feat. How can you translate cultural change to these core business competencies? Again, it all comes down to making sure your cultural ideals, that flag of values you've staked out, are lived fully and in every sphere. Here are some ideas for how to make that happen.

People

Shortly after I joined Health Monitor, I remember doing a Zoom town hall meeting for our employees (a couple of hundred people) where we allowed them to ask questions about anything and everything. And I answered their queries, transparently and honestly. Afterward, we sent out an anonymous survey asking them, "Hey, was this helpful? Is it clear where the organization is going? How do you feel? Do you have confidence in where the organization is headed? Would you recommend the organization to a friend looking for a job?"

I honestly wasn't sure what they would say. I knew it was a period of uncertainty for the company, and I knew that those uncertain periods can be cause for good people to jump ship. So I wanted to see what the mood was like. I wanted to see if those cultural changes we had been implementing were being felt by the people in the company.

I was pleasantly surprised by the outcome. We got a 92 percent positive response to the question, "I feel confident in the direction the company's going in." I remember turning to my CFO—now chief operating officer—Howard Halligan, and saying, "Hey, you know what? I know that the board of directors and our financial partners and investors probably are interested in harder metrics, like revenue, profit, and client numbers. But I actually think that this is the best metric, the best KPI, that we've seen in these first ninety days." And I meant it.

These people were having *a lot* thrown at them. We were in a period of rapid, nonstop change. But still, 92 percent of them believed in the company and where it was headed. They were excited. They were embracing those changes. They would even recommend the organization to a friend. *That* was the point when I knew we were going to succeed in taking this company to a new level of accomplishment and success. Because, as I've mentioned from the very start of this book, great change doesn't happen without great people. So knowing that we had that buy-in, that support, from our talented employees—that reassured me we were going in the right direction. It reaffirmed my optimism.

That was a really validating moment for me. In my mind, we had won the toughest metric of all—conquering people's hearts and minds and getting them on board with change. I encourage other change agents to ask themselves that question too: Do your people understand where you're going? Because you need your people at every level, not just the leadership, to see the vision. As I said before, people would rather know they're building Notre-Dame Cathedral than just chiseling stone. You also need your team to believe in the leadership. And they did. So that was a great moment for me, personally and professionally.

I believed so strongly in that metric, I made sure that it was shared with the board of directors. And, at that time, our numbers were trending consistently up. So I could have just presented them with the financial information and left it at that. But I wanted to make sure that they saw both the financial measures *and* that they got a sense for the tone in the organization—I wanted to drive home that this parallel wasn't a coincidence. Because it's not.

I firmly believe that it's the people who get the results. When you get the right people in the right place doing the right things, and they're passionate about what they're doing, the results will follow. That's why, when I create a business plan, I start with the people (and, inherently tied to that, the culture). Of course, I'm cognizant of my audience when I tell a story. If I'm presenting to a financial audience, I lead with the numbers. But I also champion cultural victories like that one. Because, in my head, it's people first, always. The rest will follow.

Process

After people, the next thing I've commonly found that needs to be tackled in organizational change is processes. And this often goes hand in hand with structural changes. For example, I previously mentioned how siloed thinking can slow down an organization, especially an organization when it's in the midst of change. So changing decision-making processes in this instance might mean taking two departments and bringing them together as one. That single structural change can streamline multiple work processes (and improve collaboration).

A change agent must examine the current structure for change opportunities. A big part of that starts with identifying value and how to best unlock it (instead of identifying the negatives and just eliminating them). Entertain hypotheticals. Think creatively. What's the ideal scenario? If you can't attain that, how close can you get?

When I've entered organizations, I've focused on creating a chain of value. So instead of silo A, silo B, and silo C, what if we created a single ABC chain of value? That could mean merging departments. It could mean eliminating departments. It could mean looking at the leadership of one department and giving them two departments to oversee. Those structural changes will, in turn, influence processes—ideally simplifying them.

One way to do this is to consider mission and purpose. Where do mission and purpose overlap? If you can find an overlap, that may be an opportunity to create a more cohesive structure and simplify your processes.

For example, at Health Monitor, one of the first things we did in the initial ninety days of my tenure was to combine our network sales and operations departments. Why? Because they shared the same mission—nurturing positive relationships with physicians.

Basically, the service team maintains the valuable relationship the network sales pros have built. Before a screen gets onto the physician's office wall, we have to go to that physician's office and talk to them about the educational value of our products. The network sales professionals are the field team that goes out, initiates contact with healthcare professionals, and has those conversations. Then we have the service department—another field team. Their job is to call on physicians' offices where we already have screens, ensuring their technology is working and finding out whether they're happy with the product.

When I arrived at Health Monitor, these two teams were in separate departments. We decided we could bring more value to our clients (and streamline our operational processes) if we took the sales piece and the service piece and brought them together in one single field organization. Whether it was selling to a new office or maintaining a good relationship with an existing office, the aim was the same—to nurture positive relationships with physicians. Bringing together these two components thus felt like a logical step.

Of course, these kinds of changes mean changing the scaffolding of the company. For example, if once there were two department heads, there's probably going to be only one moving forward. Changing the scaffolding means making tough decisions. But, in the long term, it's in the best interests of the company—and, most importantly, in the best interests of the clients and the customers.

Pet projects are another common thing I've seen throughout my career that can gum up a company's internal processes. I call them skunkworks projects. Different individuals or teams start working on their little pet projects—whether that's a new product or a campaign or service—independently of one another. The problem is that when you have everyone focusing on their own small project, you don't have the full weight of the organization to support that project.

As a result, every skunkworks project tends to move slowly. It can also be a distraction from the organization's larger vision. Some of those pet projects aren't even in the bigger interests of the organization. People get so caught up in their passion projects, they lose sight of the big picture. So it's often on you, as a leader, to identify and cut those skunkworks projects, especially those that don't align with the cultural values of the organization.

Those kinds of structure- and process-related decisions are the ones that require bravery, but they're also the ones that can yield big results. It requires a willingness to reach in and poke at some comfortable, well-established attitudes of "This is the way we do things." It also requires some imagination. You have to be able to envision that there might be *better* ways to do things. You then have to convince others of that vision.

Products

Finally, with your people and processes defined on the inside, you can start looking at what you're actually putting *out* into the world: products. I've already written at length about my personal experience when it comes to revamping products at Health Monitor. The only additional note I'll make now—one that could serve you   is to say this: when considering products, always remember your audience.

That's been our guiding light at Health Monitor, and it's served us well. The birth control lesson from chapter 1 is a prime example. We were creating info guides for young college-aged women about birth control options, and we were thinking of creating *printed* patient guides. Then, of course, we realized that college-aged women weren't going to walk across campus with a printed magazine (I knew from my own experience as a dad that my daughters wouldn't be caught dead doing it!). So we pivoted: we created an interactive app instead, with videos, quizzes, and more. It was the right decision—the right decision for our company and our client, and (most importantly) for our audience.

I don't know what kinds of products your company provides, so I can't give you much more granular advice than that. But there is one more point I want to make: be gracious with yourself when it comes to product research and development. R&D takes time. It means coming up with a genius idea, trying it out, and then discovering that it wasn't such a genius idea after all. It's better to pull back than to rush something to market that isn't ready.

Also, particularly when it comes to the product component, beware that there may be external factors beyond your control that can impact timelines and outcomes. This book I'm writing? I'll have finished it by September 2022. When will I get a copy in my hand? Mid-2023. Paper shortages and logistics hurdles are at stake. Those are things I can't control. So I've got to accept that (and look forward to getting my hands on that hard copy when I can).

Urgency is important to organizational transformation, something I'll speak on further in the next chapter. But sometimes there will be roadblocks that slow you down, roadblocks you can't control. In those moments, I'd say it's more important than ever to fall back on those cultural values you staked out. And when you *do* get the win—when that product is launched or gets market authorization or whatever the case may be—celebrate it!

For example, at Health Monitor, we embarked on an initiative to get our entire digital network platform certified by an independent auditor. And we thought the process would take exactly twenty-four weeks. That was the timeline we had set out. Well, it took longer. It ended up taking twenty-eight weeks. Fifteen years ago, I would have viewed that as a failure. I would have fixated on those lost four weeks. What took so long? Why were we behind? What was the holdup? How could we speed things up?

But that kind of attitude would have contributed to a culture of negativity. And by that point in my career, I knew better. I knew that power could be found in positivity. I knew that this was a big win. I knew this kind of certification process was a major undertaking that could well take five months, six months, or more. But we had to get it done. And we got it done! It was part of our larger blueprint, part of our plan to get us to where we needed to be. So we carried on. And in the end, even though it took twenty-eight weeks instead of twenty-four weeks, we celebrated that win, together.

Find the North Point on Your Compass (and Keep the Course)

In every experience I've had as a change agent, transformation has required a cultural shift backed by strong, clearly defined values. Defining those values requires an honest self-assessment. I think that first step, that initial self-assessment, can make or break a transformation journey. That self-assessment ultimately turns out to define the vision of the company going forward—where are we now, where do we want to be, and how are we going to get there? I like to call it the north point of the company's compass. Some might also call it a blueprint for change.

In the introduction, I spoke about how we developed that kind of blueprint at Razorfish, bringing together thirty-five functional leaders at an all-day off-site meeting. I gave each person there a compass, a symbolic representation of our mission for the day—to define the north point for Razorfish and to articulate the course we wanted to take. We spent the day in breakout sessions, having honest conversations about the agency, where it was at, where we wanted it to be, and how we were going to get there. That meeting was full of tough discussions, but it also became the kick-start moment where I (and my entire leadership team) committed to enacting fundamental change at Razorfish.

At Health Monitor, the journey was similar. We started by defining our north point—the need to pivot from a legacy print publisher to a modern digital-first media agency. This had become especially critical in the face of the COVID-19 pandemic. That north point then guided all our decisions going forward, from trashing the old office desk phones to getting more transparent about our physician office network with our client agencies.

Without the cultural component, you run the risk of losing your north point and letting your ship steer off course or lose momentum.

How you define your north point—that's up to you. Those are only a couple of examples. Earlier I outlined some key components, including some ubiquitous sticking points that often need to be addressed in organizational transformations. But when you define that north point, don't ignore the culture component. Better yet, prioritize it. When you plant that flag of cultural ideals, you are setting the tone for the entire transformation journey.

Without the cultural component, you run the risk of losing your north point and letting your ship steer off course or lose momentum. You've got to define those cultural touchstones, implement them practically, and communicate them constantly, in both word and action.

And that job of communicating falls to a person I like to call the storyteller-in-chief, a role I'll get into in the next chapter. This is the individual who helps to articulate and reiterate the organization's cultural values throughout a change journey. Their role is critical to staying the course.

CHAPTER 4

COMMUNICATION

By not only *defining* but also *living out* your cultural values, you can make great strides toward transforming your organization. And if you keep your north point in mind through it all, you'll stay on course. But beware: there is a real danger of losing course when you're enacting a big transformation. Because business transformation is inherently complicated and multifaceted. You might be changing everything from department structures to technology, workflows, people, and more. In the previous chapter, I touched on a few common points of friction that often need a revamp, but that list is by no means exhaustive.

I should also note that the points I've identified in the previous chapter don't necessarily apply to your organization. Maybe one or two of them do, maybe none of them do (in which case, congrats, you don't need to finish reading this book!). But, as mentioned, in my years of experience, these are some of the most salient points that need addressing in most business transformation processes.

If these core building blocks aren't in place or dealt with, making meaningful, lasting changes will be difficult, uncomfortable, or downright impossible.

All of the points I've just flagged share one key component: they help to build trust. Cut down siloes? More trust. Improve transparency? More trust. Eliminate negativity? More trust. Empower your people? Trust. Clarify your processes? Trust. Improve your products? Trust! Trust, both within the company and beyond, is essential for a successful change to occur.

> If the first step in enacting meaningful change is planting the culture flag, identifying and enacting a core set of values, the second step is communicating those values.

Here's the thing: that trust starts with trust in a strong leader, the person you might think of as the change agent or, as I like to refer to the role, the storyteller-in-chief. This is a job that frequently falls to the CEO. It's the responsibility of whoever is at the helm of the organization. The leader needs to be an example of the core cultural narrative within a transforming organization. They need to foster stories that confirm the values of an organization in flux, affirming transparency and establishing trust in the process.

If the first step in enacting meaningful change is planting the culture flag, identifying and enacting a core set of values, the second step is communicating those values. And that's where my idea of the storyteller-in-chief comes into the picture. As a leader, you can't scribble down those core values on a piece of paper, stick it in your desk drawer, and never glance at it again. You've got to communicate those values—with great intensity, consistency, and clarity—to the people in your organization.

Setting the Tone: The Leader's Role as the Storyteller-in-Chief

I want to start with a hard-to-stomach truth about being the storyteller-in-chief: it requires accepting that things won't always go to plan. I know this from personal experience. Not everything in business (or in life) goes to plan. I didn't want to write a book suggesting otherwise, which is why I've been candid about both my personal and my professional struggles. I don't want to suggest that I started into the business world right after graduating Hamilton College and began simply climbing the ranks, each day sunnier, brighter, and more perfect than the next. And I don't want to suggest that my various roles as a storyteller-in-chief were always an upward climb to the top of the mountain.

On the contrary, when I first arrived at Health Monitor, I set some competitive—you might even call them audacious—goals. Guess what? We didn't meet them all. Not even close, in some cases. I remember, early on, we had a sort of poor-performing financial quarter. It was the first quarter that I was CEO, as we were trying to see through this transformation and grapple with the impact of COVID-19. I had planted my flag of core values for the company: initiative, teamwork, and (gulp) *transparency*. It was time to live out my values and bluntly communicate the underwhelming financial figures.

So the senior leadership team and I shared those first somewhat underwhelming results. But I wasn't defeated by that. I told everyone, "Hey, it's our first quarter together, and we're putting these building blocks for change in place—but things don't change overnight. No, the results aren't what we want them to be. But we'll get there. And it's important that we're open about that." I was conscious that I had to set the tone, and I refused to let that be a negative tone.

I may have been met with some skepticism (or flat-out disbelief—I'm not sure which). People probably already thought I was a little nuts, taking over the CEO role in a pandemic. Now they might have thought I was really crazy. So I tried to explain why I wasn't getting hung up on those numbers. And I wound up sharing a personal story with the team—which I'll share with you now and which I come back to often when the transformation journey gets tough.

After my wife passed, there was a period of time when I was a single parent. I was at home with my high school–aged son, a freshman, and the first thing I did for him was to buy him a giant battle flag that said, "Don't give up the ship." Every US Navy ship sails under several flags, an American flag, a US Navy flag, and a "Don't give up the ship" flag. Those words are attributed to James Lawrence, a navy captain commanding the USS *Chesapeake* in the War of 1812. On June 1, 1813, the USS *Chesapeake* and the British HMS *Shannon* were locked in a fight, during which Lawrence was shot. He ended up dying of his wounds. One of his final commands: Don't give up the ship.

So I got my son this giant battle flag that says, "Don't give up the ship." He hung it on his wall, and it became this huge metaphor for him of not giving up—not quitting. That flag made it to college too, but before he graduated, he took the flag down. By that time, he didn't need it anymore. It was there in a moment when the world was really rocky for him, when he needed that reminder as he grappled with the uncertainties of his mom's passing. It had done its job.

That's the story I shared with my senior leadership team as we looked at those financial figures from our first quarter together. And that's the story I'm sharing with you now, because I think those words are a reminder that every storyteller-in-chief can use in their business transformation journey. Those words are a reminder every *person* can use in their *life* journey. Sometimes we all need that reminder: don't give up the ship. Anyone who tells you otherwise is, I'd guess, lying (to you or to themselves). Keep your eye on that north point on your compass, whether in business or in life at large, and keep going. Remember, grit carries the day.

Communicating a Consistent Message: How a Storyteller-in-Chief Stays on Course

As a storyteller-in-chief, you've got to be prepared to move quickly and maintain momentum. And you've got to ensure that others are keeping the pace too. That means communicating your message, your change values, with great consistency, regularity, and urgency. In my past experiences, one way I've done this was with company-wide emails, sent every two weeks, with a short narrative about the company's progress and obstacles (and how we were going to get around those obstacles).

At Health Monitor, I also used those monthly CEO videos I've mentioned previously—the ones that had me sitting on the edge of my desk, in jeans, giving an update on what was going on with the company: "Hey, here's the latest on our financial performance. Here are the new products we're launching. Here are some of the new clients we're working with. Here's the update on the latest internal changes (and why we made them). Here are some of the new people we're hiring to help us grow." And so on.

The visual component of a video format was important to me. I felt it was an opportunity to give people a sense not only of the revised mission, the digital transformation of the company, but also of my personal style as a CEO, of my own commitment to the core values I'd planted that flag for—transparency, initiative, and teamwork. Also, the videos could best communicate the sense of urgency and the speed with which we were asking people to pick up the pace—because speed is critical to transformational success and to maintaining a competitive advantage (something I'll go into greater detail on in the next chapter).

Those CEO videos I've mentioned were sent out to the whole company according to a regularly cadenced schedule, issued every three to four weeks. We wanted to make sure to maintain regularity. We didn't want it to be a one-off thing. It's like subscribing to a podcast: if you're going to start listening to a new series, and you get just a couple of episodes in and then it stops, you're going to get pretty annoyed. That's the last thing we wanted.

> **I've found that the more on-message and frequent your communications as the storyteller-in-chief are, the better.**

By thinking of those CEO videos as a regular podcast, something to keep adding episodes to, I was able to reinforce our transformation journey. I could consistently communicate those core values I'd defined from the start and show how we were upholding them. I've found that the more on-message and frequent your communications as the storyteller-in-chief are, the better.

People learn and change their habits through repetition and application. And, as I've mentioned, for companies to change, the people within them need to change or make changes. It's up to the storyteller-in-chief to lead that charge. With great consistency, a skilled storyteller can also help evangelize change in a way. Think about it: a spiritual or religious person doesn't just practice their faith for a few days of the year. A devout Christian doesn't just go to church on Easter and Christmas. They go every Sunday.

That's the kind of consistency you need if you're going to be a successful storyteller-in-chief, one who can lead meaningful, lasting change. This is especially true in companies that have stagnated or that are very set in their ways—the kinds of companies that are rooted in the we've-always-done-it-*this*-way attitude. If you want to enact transformation in that context, you've got to very sincerely and consistently preach your change message.

You also need to be honest about it. I hate to break it to you, but that means being honest about the good and the bad. (Unfortunately, being honest about the bad seems to be a pitfall for some companies.) Because if you're not honest and that gets out, you've effectively shattered trust. Moving forward from that will be very, very hard.

A CEO who adopts that storyteller-in-chief hat is a little bit like a download bar on your phone. When you're downloading a new app or media file to your phone, you get that little bar on the screen, visually showing the download's progress. An honest storyteller-in-chief is like that download bar. Some weeks, the message may be good; the "download"—the change journey—is clicking along! Other weeks, the message may be "Oops, something went wrong; we've got to start this download again." Another week, the movement on the progress bar may be paused, and you've just got to wait a bit.

Maintaining that kind of honesty can be daunting for a leader, even very experienced leaders. However, I do think it's essential and, ultimately, for the best. Why? A storyteller-in-chief who approaches their role with great candor can still continue to successfully preach their change message because they'll maintain trust. And without trust, true change isn't possible.

Keeping the Pace: How to Maintain Momentum as the Storyteller-in-Chief

I personally believe that a successful business transformation can be instituted only with some sense of urgency. What's more, sometimes you don't have a *choice* but to act quickly. Transformation must often be done at a rapid pace. Maybe the shareholders are clamoring for increased profits by X date, for example, or maybe the company is hemorrhaging clients, or employees are quitting in droves because of a poor work culture.

These are just a few examples of the types of high-pressure circumstances organizations may be under when they decide transformation is necessary. In those time-sensitive transformation projects, it becomes all the more important to clearly enunciate the cultural values that will inform organizational evolution—and to reiterate them, ensuring that you keep your eye on that north point on the compass.

Even if that pressure isn't there, speed is still essential in the transformation process, in my experience. Anytime I've been asked to enact change in my career, be it within an individual team or department, or for a company as a whole, I've found that there's a certain magic to speed. That first ninety-day window is really critical. I know that there are older (and, I would argue, dated) frameworks that require new chief executives to spend the first ninety days doing due diligence. But, for me, in those first ninety days, you not only need to do due diligence—but also you need to act.

Only through action can you demonstrate that you're actually *embracing* a culture change, not just talking about a culture change. In my first ninety days at Health Monitor, there were organizational changes. There were structural changes. There were new product changes. There were changes to our relationships with our vendors and clients. There were infrastructure changes, from eliminating desk phones to painting over reserved parking spaces. We changed the company's branding, logo, and website. We changed the nomenclature we used to talk about the company. We created a new social media engagement platform. We created a ton of thought leadership material for the industry, to help raise our profile and share our knowledge.

Now we could have spent ninety days doing due diligence and *then* made all those changes. But why? If you see something on day one that needs changing (like a numbered parking space), why wait? You don't need to abide by that antiquated business rule book from the 1980s. Because guess what? We're not in the 1980s anymore! In transformation, speed becomes an unspoken cultural value. That sense of urgency is even more critical in modern businesses, whether you're in advertising or in media or you're making pharmaceuticals or bars of soap. The world evolves more quickly these days, and businesses need to evolve more quickly to keep up.

Pace is important. When you're taking on the role of the change agent (or the storyteller-in-chief), it's on you to set the pace. But you've got to accept that the pace of change will vary. I like to compare it to a long-distance run. I've done a lot of long-distance running and completed a bunch of half marathons. As you train and prepare for that kind of grueling race, you develop a mile marker. You set a goal for how fast you're going to clock each mile in that race, be it eight minutes or nine minutes or whatever (the older I get, the bigger those numbers get).

So when I start a race, I know I can run at a certain clip every mile, because that's what I've been training at. And it's great to have that mile marker. You need it to regulate your pace. It can help you achieve your personal best. But it's also not something you're going to hit every time. Some miles are a little more uphill. Some miles you're a little thirstier than others. And, as a result, you end up with better and worse mile times. Some are faster. Some are slower. If you're running on an especially hot September day, on an uphill stretch, you might not hit that eight-minute mile marker you set for yourself *in that stretch*. And that's okay.

It doesn't mean you quit. It just means you accept the fact that mile seven was a little slower than you thought and then you try to get back on pace on mile eight. We all have those mile sevens. The point is, you're still tracking toward the goal, toward the finish line. I think understanding that and showing yourself some forgiveness, some grace, is really important. That's a lesson that I've found applies both in business and in life at large. For example, the career of a successful businessperson generally unfolds over years, usually decades. Yes, every single day matters. Yes, speed matters. However, it's important to keep the big picture in mind. Just keep that north point on your compass and keep moving.

That said, sometimes even that—*keep moving*—is a challenge. How do you avoid getting stuck? If you've got a big decision to make, for example, how do you make it with the speed needed while still giving it the due consideration it deserves? For this, I like to use the one-way versus two-way door analogy.

One-Way or Two-Way Door: How to Make Quick Decisions in Business (or in Life at Large)

Speed is important for meaningful transformation. Without some sense of urgency, I've found that people and organizations alike tend to get stuck, often mired down in the details. The solution? I suggest having a bias toward action. Don't get hung up on extensive analysis. In the famous words of Nike: Just do it.

Easier said than done, right? Especially if you're the designated storyteller-in-chief. You don't want to be the one responsible for making the wrong move and steering the ship off course, away from that north point on the compass. Analysis, indecision, contemplation—they all feel inevitable, especially when you're shifting such core business components as people, products, and processes.

I used to struggle with this immensely. In the introduction, I mentioned how a work friend had nicknamed me the Senator. Because, he said, like a good senator, I could stake out both sides of any argument: it could be this, *or* it could be that. Well, that diplomacy could also lead to endless debate, which takes up a lot of time. After my own personal hardships, losing my parents and my wife in a short period, I became keenly aware of just how precious time is. And I changed. I no longer wanted to extensively debate every decision in my life. I wanted to take action, quickly and confidently. But how?

There's an easy trick I started using to help me make business decisions fast (and it works for personal decisions too, in case you're grappling with any of those): the one-way versus two-way door. I try to frame all decisions as either a one-way or a two-way door. A one-way door opens only one way, right? Once you step through that door, there's no going back. So if a decision is a one-way door decision, it better be sound. Something like firing an employee—that's a one-way door decision. You can't go back on it. You can't change your mind and walk back through the door.

But then there are the two-way doors. You can step out—but you can also come back in. A product launch can be a two-way door decision. You can launch a product—but you can also pull it off the market. You can adapt it as needed. And then you can even launch it again.

Once you start using that scheme, you'll quicky discover that the vast majority of decisions are, in fact, two-way doors. In most cases, there is a way to change, adapt, pivot, or go in a different direction. It's not a once-and-for-all final decision. And isn't that a reassuring thought?

So that's the mindset I use when making decisions. That mindset helps support urgency, but it also encourages you to really consider a decision carefully when it counts. I've certainly learned that the place to be a little more thoughtful is on those one-way doors. Because in those instances, once you've made the decision, it's done. There's no going back.

Empowered Leaders as Pacesetters: How a Strong Leadership Team Keeps Momentum

I don't just use the one-way versus two-way door analogy myself. I encourage others in the organizations I've worked in to use it too. When someone approaches me with a problem, something requiring a choice, I ask them, "Okay, is it a one-way or a two-way door?" If we take this action, is there a means of retreat? Can we go back and do it differently later? Or will we be stuck on one side of the door (hopefully not the wrong side)? And I trust my leadership team to make the right choice.

That brings me to another point when it comes to maintaining momentum: you can't do it alone. You can *try*. But, odds are, you'll fail. And you'll get pretty exhausted pretty quickly. I mean, running might seem like a solitary act, but even a distance runner has help— people giving them water along the course, for example, or cheering them on.

When Eliud Kipchoge broke the two-hour marathon barrier in Vienna, Austria, in 2019, he didn't do it alone. He had a whole team of people doing everything from making sure he had the right shoes to measuring the wind resistance and checking the smoothness of the track. He also had a team of pacemakers, also known as pacesetters. There are runners who would jump in alongside him, running with him to make sure he held the fast pace he needed to achieve his goal. They also provided psychological support.

As a storyteller-in-chief, you need your own team of pacesetters. And that means empowering other leaders in your organization. One way to do this is to give them more agency. For example, in the previous chapter, I mentioned our on-the-spot bonus program at Health Monitor. A manager could decide, on the spot, to award someone a bonus if they saw them doing something right at work. It didn't need to be checked by me or by HR or by anyone else. I trusted my team to recognize those actions worthy of some extra accolades and to assign those bonuses as warranted.

Of course, empowering your leadership team requires trust, which means you want to have the right leaders in place. On this note, when it comes to getting the right people in an organization, my adage is be slow to decide and quick to act. The "Be slow" part means you should give people an opportunity to demonstrate their skills and competencies as well as their possible weaknesses—areas that could use development. The "Be quick" part means, once you've seen those strengths and weaknesses, you have to take action. If someone isn't right for a role, you have to make that change without delay. Because delay hampers change and that harms your organization.

Now that doesn't necessarily mean getting rid of people (no boardroom "You're fired!" moments needed). Sometimes it's about elevating people. Quick to act can be this: "Hey, this person needs to be promoted and given more responsibility or a different responsibility." We've seen many great examples of this at Health Monitor, some of which I've mentioned previously, like William Saint-Louis, who went from dealing with more routine IT issues to becoming our executive vice president, chief technology and digital operations officer and overseeing our next generation of 5G screen development.

Dan Tassone is a similar case. He was second-in-command in our campaign deployment department. We realized that he knew so much about the health of our network and how the offices interacted with the technology, we made him our executive vice president, chief network health and strategy officer (a role he holds today). That allowed him to oversee the engagement with the physician offices *and* the engagement with the technology. It was about lifting him up from a more day-to-day tactical job into a more strategic role, one that was a much better fit for him. He benefitted and so did the company. That's just one example of how empowering your leadership and trusting them can reap rewards.

Now if you want to build the strongest team of pacesetters possible, you've got to learn how to assess each person and work with them based on where they are. That's something I've learned from teaching. For the past ten years, I've served as an adjunct faculty member at a business school in Philadelphia. Every year, I teach a marketing class in their executive MBA program. Some of these MBA students are right out of undergrad, barely twenty-three years old, while others have twenty-plus years of work experience and well-developed professional careers. And one of the things I've learned is that you have to meet each student where they are. The same goes for people within a company, especially when you're setting up your leadership team—your pacesetters.

You'll then be able to empower that senior leadership team so that they all are *truly* leaders. I don't micromanage, nor do I want to. I truly trust the people who work directly for me, the senior leadership team. They can all make decisions. They can make change happen. They have the blueprint that everyone has agreed on and aligned with. They know the north point on the compass, and they have the map for how to get there. They are critical in achieving that shared vision. And you probably won't achieve it without them. So I think letting them have the authority—to give out bonuses, to make hires, whatever it may be—is essential.

Those pieces of empowerment help make stronger leaders. And every storyteller-in-chief needs to be supported by strong leaders. Because, like Kipchoge's pacesetters, they aren't just there to help spur along the transformation. They are also psychological cheerleaders. That's something I've found invaluable in my own experiences as a storyteller-in-chief.

I get my energy from other people. With that in mind, one of the things that I found helpful during the transformation process at Health Monitor was getting the entire leadership team together physically. Even though, officially, the company was working remote, we brought the leadership team together so that we would check in on one another. We had these regularly cadenced meetings, on a biweekly basis, and we still have them. It keeps me and the rest of my team motivated. We know, "Hey, we're going to get together in two weeks. I want to have progress to show when that time comes." And that applies to everyone around the table. In a way, we feed off each other's energy. That energy, enthusiasm, and forward progress just gets reinforced every two weeks and keeps us on track.

Especially during the early days of the company's transformation journey, that was invaluable. It was an essential reminder to me, and to all of us, that the transformation journey wasn't a solo race. We were running together. Given how daunting some changes can be, and sometimes overwhelming or downright scary, that's a huge benefit.

Leading from the Front: How to Build Resilience as the Storyteller-in-Chief

When you have your north point on your compass, you want to get there as soon as possible. But there will be setbacks. This is, in my experience, inevitable in any transformation journey. (If you've managed a transformation journey without any setbacks, then *you* should be writing a book.) The thing is, those setbacks tend to slow down the pace of transformation, and this is where many organizations tend to get stuck.

Ultimately, it's the storyteller-in-chief's job to maintain momentum in the face of those setbacks. Yes, you have your pacesetters alongside you. But you're the one who's first deciding, "Okay, how fast are we going to run this mile?" You're setting the tone and the pace. That brings an added responsibility with it: you also have a responsibility to nurture resilience and to say, "Hey, we're going to face hurdles and that's okay." If they fall, you want to get your team back on their feet and across the finish line.

I touched on this briefly at the start of this chapter, when I discussed that underwhelming financial quarter at Health Monitor— my first as the company's CEO. I shared that personal anecdote with my leadership team about the navy flag I'd given my son after his mom's passing: don't give up the ship. Those words are all about resilience, right? Of course pithy mottoes alone can't build resilience. What *can* help is identifying wins. In the face of failures and setbacks, point to what's going well.

I wrote in the previous chapter about how pleased I was by our employee survey, in which 92 percent of respondents said they had confidence in the company's trajectory. That was a BIG (yes, all-caps-worthy BIG) win for us. I also mentioned how we got our entire digital network platform certified by an independent auditor (the process we thought would take twenty-four weeks but took twenty-eight). Well, despite that delay, when we got that news, we celebrated! It was a major milestone. A little later than hoped for, yes, but we still got there. My point is that reiterating the good stuff, the positives, the wins, is critical if you're going to foster resilience and keep your organization on track during a change journey.

Another way to nurture resilience and keep people motivated is to lead from the front. Get in the trenches with your people. Just because the moniker is storyteller-in-chief doesn't mean that you're only telling the story. You've also got to take action.

You can't expect your people to be personally invested in a change journey if you aren't personally invested in the change journey. For example, I personally make a point of meeting with clients at Health Monitor at least three times per week. I mean, first of all, I love it. I don't want to just sit behind my desk at the office and have other people report to me about those client meetings. How boring is that? I want to be there, in the room, talking pitches and brainstorming ideas.

But getting involved in this way—leading from the front—also fosters that sense of teamwork that's so important to a broader organizational change. You want your people to know, "Whether we succeed or fail, we do it as a group." It's about being part of the team.

It's about being part of the entourage, part of the cast. It's about having people know that the CEO is not in some unapproachable office in some remote corner somewhere but that they are *out there*—with the employees, on the front lines, going to see customers. That builds a sense of teamwork.

> **A great storyteller-in-chief is, as dramatic as this sounds, ready to fall on the grenade and be held accountable for both the wins and the losses.**

It also shows that the CEO is willing to accept accountability (and, let's be real, not all of them are). By putting yourself out there and leading from the front, you are opening yourself up to being held accountable. In some ways, it's easier to sit tucked away in your office and just review the results as they come in, right? You don't have to be held personally responsible for something like an unhappy client if you weren't ever in the room with that client. But that is, in my experience, not a path toward positive or effective change.

A great storyteller-in-chief is, as dramatic as this sounds, ready to fall on the grenade and be held accountable for both the wins and the losses. The role of storyteller-in-chief can't be passed off or out-sourced. It's not about putting somebody else on the line. It's about leading from the front. And that will help nurture resilience, both your own and your team's. It will help build that grit I talked about in the introduction to this book. And grit is what you need to succeed in business and in life.

Remember, according to Angela Duckworth's research, published in her book *Grit*, success doesn't come from determinants like family status, wealth, or IQ (although, of course, those things can help—let's be real). However, in most cases, success comes from your willingness to get knocked down, pick yourself back up, and keep moving. It comes from resilience. It comes from an adamant, stubborn tenacity—the belief that, no matter what, you don't give up the ship.

Know Your Role as the Storyteller-in-Chief (and Honor It)

The role of storyteller-in-chief is a big responsibility. You've got to stake out those clear culture values and set that north point on the compass to follow. You've got to communicate your change plan, with consistency and urgency. And you've got to be transparent and honest about the transformation journey, both its current status and where it's going. Start there, and you'll build trust—your team can trust you and you can trust them. And then it becomes a "we" story, not a "me" story, where you can all run the gauntlet of the transformation race (and cross the finish line) together.

Clear and consistent communication is how you solve that people part of the equation, winning people's hearts and minds and convincing them to join you on the change journey. Look, transformation journeys aren't always easy (or fun). Believe me, it gets a lot easier and more enjoyable when you've got the support of a great team by your side. And by communicating your change message, by evangelizing it *and* living it, you'll be able to get your team on board. And that will add up to an engaged and enthusiastic team. A team that's prepared to see through the change journey. A team that won't give up the ship.

Beyond that, communication isn't just about winning over other people. It's also what's going to keep *you*, the storyteller-in-chief, on track. Reiterating your cultural values and revisiting your change journey map will remind you to keep your eyes set on the north point on the compass. It will hold you accountable and keep you motivated. It will help you maintain confidence in your journey and where you're headed. It will nurture resilience, for both you and your team.

And, as I've mentioned, that resilience is essential. Because when an organization undertakes a major transformation, *things won't go to plan*. Let me say it again: Things. Will. Not. Go. To. Plan. Annoying, right? Here I am, telling you that you just need those three Cs to achieve effective transformation (culture, communication, and competitive advantage). At the same time, I'm telling you that, even with those three Cs, things won't work out exactly like you expect them to. Well, that's the honest truth, and I can't sugarcoat it.

But my point is this: by building transformation on the basis of strong cultural values and by communicating those values, and your change journey, with urgency and consistency, you greatly increase your odds of success. You're far more likely to actually achieve the transformation you're seeking. You're more likely to become a company that can easily evolve, that can pivot, that can change direction when needed. You're more likely to develop a company that's agile and adaptable. A company that's forward thinking.

And all of that will help you maintain one major asset: your competitive advantage. Let's face it, transformation in the business world is usually made with an eye toward keeping or gaining a competitive edge. Logically, this will always be a consideration in any transformation journey. The good news? There are some steps companies can take during transformation to harness or improve their competitiveness—and that's what I'm going to talk about next.

CHAPTER 5

COMPETITIVE ADVANTAGE

Transformation usually has a purpose. People don't bother going through the effort of making great changes if they're not going to achieve a certain outcome. When the hordes hit the gym on January 1, it's usually because they want to improve their health, or lose weight, or run a marathon. I can't know what a particular individual's personal motivation may be in that context. But in the business world, in my experience, transformation is usually a question of maintaining or regaining a competitive advantage.

Every organization that I've accompanied on a change journey has had competitiveness in mind. In some cases, it's been the central goal. In other cases, it's been secondary to other goals. Regardless, the successful change journeys I've witnessed have all had one thing in common, one thing that has allowed them to maintain (or attain) that competitive edge—they are always, *always* keeping the customer in mind. The truly great companies have a customer-centric focus that I'd say verges on obsession.

P&G, where I got my start, is a great example. This is a company that literally sends teams into consumers' homes to find out how they're using paper towels and toilet tissue so that they can then better adapt those products to the consumers' needs. They genuinely want to know their customers and how to best serve them. And that's part of the reason why, in my opinion, P&G has stood the test of time (the company was established in 1837, when candlemaker William Procter and soap maker James Gamble merged their businesses in Cincinnati).

> **The truly great companies have a customer-centric focus that I'd say verges on obsession.**

On the other side of the equation, you can see companies that didn't respond to the call of the customer. I mentioned a few of these in the introduction. Kodak failed to embrace digital when consumers wanted it. Blackberry failed to adapt their device fast enough to compete with the iPhone's sleek touchscreen design, which consumers went wild for when it appeared on the scene. Blockbuster didn't pivot fast enough to keep up with the demand for streaming services. Those companies are still around, yes, but they're a far cry from the industry leaders they once were.

The question is, How do you avoid the same fate? If you're going to maintain a competitive advantage through transformation, there are three key points you've got to address: you've got to create a superior product; you've got to get obsessed with your customer; and you've got to constantly be open to change. In this chapter, I explain how to hit all three of those points. I also look at point-of-care marketing as a case study, examining how the industry has managed to maintain its competitive edge by adhering to precisely these three points.

Create a Superior Product

Some companies think that a competitive advantage is all about the *brand*, a concept that has become almost sacrosanct in recent decades. With the right brand, people think all things are possible: with the right brand, you'll sell the most, gain the most followers, enjoy the most loyalty! If only. Yes, branding matters. It can make a difference, helping companies connect with their target audiences and binding them more closely, boosting their loyalty. But it's not the starting point in achieving a competitive edge, especially in transformation processes.

Here's a dirty little secret from somebody who's been in advertising for thirty-five years: it's not the advertising. The ads aren't what make you succeed. The advertising comes last. First, you develop the superior, differentiated product. And then you can create your memorable ad campaigns—and they'll actually *work*, because they're promoting a product that works. But without a superior product to back it up, a great ad campaign won't get you far.

Ideally, you'll have an "irresistibly superior" product. That's a term famously used by P&G CEO Jon R. Moeller. According to his concept, you want to have irresistibly superior products so that when the consumer is faced with an economic choice, given the macroeconomic conditions, they will still choose the P&G brand on the shelf—even if it costs more. And the consumer will choose that pricier brand with confidence and without regret, without any qualms that they're paying more, because they *know* that it's superior.

The irresistibly superior product is an ethos that continually guides P&G's product development. As a rule, P&G rigorously tests their products, at their lab north of their Cincinnati headquarters. A 2022 Bloomberg article illuminated the rigorous process that goes into testing new dishwasher products: "Employees wearing safety goggles make mac and cheese and other sticky foods to test how well Cascade strips gunk off plates in the facility's 72 dishwashers, which represent the models found in 80% of US homes."[14]

P&G used this approach to reinvigorate its Cascade dishwashing products with a series of upgrades in 2022. And those upgrades didn't just consist of updating a logo and changing some packaging. Thanks to their meticulous R&D process, P&G did a beautiful job revitalizing Cascade, even at a time when people were hesitant to run their dishwashers every night because they wanted to reduce energy use and water waste. P&G figured out what customers wanted and they delivered—by developing a dishwasher tablet that could be used in energy-efficient washers, the kinds that use less water, and still get everything clean.

Of course, P&G followed up their new Cascade product launch with some cheeky advertising, a campaign line about how they "do it every night" (run their dishwasher every night). But they had the goods, literally, to back it up. They had the superior product. That kind of clever advertising is the last step in the value chain. It comes after the superior product has been developed. And only then will it work.

I think that anecdote speaks to the power of irresistible superiority, and I think that's a concept that can be applied across all industries. If you're an attorney in Des Moines, Iowa, how do you become the go-to attorney in Des Moines, Iowa? If you're a patisserie chef in Paris, France, how do you become the go-to patisserie chef in Paris, France? If you offer cleaning services in Austin, Texas, how do you become the go-to cleaning provider in Austin, Texas?

---

14   Daniela Sirtori-Cortina, "P&G Just Wants You to Use Your Dishwasher," Bloomberg, August 1, 2022, https://www.bloomberg.com/news/features/2022-08-01/doing-dishes-in-the-dishwasher-saves-water-is-p-g-s-cascade-ad-campaign.

Whatever your industry, I think it all starts with asking yourself that question: "Am I offering an irresistibly superior product or service?" Have you differentiated your offering from the competition in a way that will attract consumers to *your* product or service, even if you're charging more than the competition? If you're P&G, and you're charging twenty-five cents more for a tube of toothpaste than an off-brand competitor, why is your tube of toothpaste worth that extra quarter? If every other lawyer in Des Moines charges $400 an hour and you charge $425, why are you worth that extra $25?

It all comes down to creating something tangible, where the end user can say, "I see the value in this service/product." Sometimes people mistakenly think that advertising is the way they'll get people to pay more for their services. For example, if you're the most expensive lawyer in Des Moines, you might think you'll make it work by putting up a billboard on the freeway. And that billboard might help generate a rush of business in the short term, sure. But, long term, you've got a reputation to sustain. And that will come from proving that your legal services are better than those of the other lawyers in town. The advertising is the last step.

Regardless of the industry, my counsel to anyone would be to always go back and say, "What is it about the product or the service that I'm offering that makes it superior? How can I make it different, better than the rest?" And during that phase, don't worry about what you or anyone else will say about it. Don't worry about where you'll promote it. Don't worry about your advertising budget. Just create the superior product. If you start there, you'll have a good chance of attaining a competitive advantage.

That's certainly an ethos that has worked for Health Monitor and that has helped us maintain our status as one of the top two largest players in our industry. We don't worry about whether our advertising budget is the biggest. It's not. What I really want to spend my time, focus, and energy, on is this: Are my products superior? Are they fantastic? Are they going to get my customer base excited?

That's why we continue to view ourselves as a content education company, first and foremost. It's why we create materials using a team of expert healthcare journalists. It's why we have our KOLs from our Medical Advisory Board review our content and give it the final sign-off. It's why we partner with organizations like the American Heart Association to corroborate our content, ensuring that it's verifiable and accurate. We want to guarantee that our products are irresistibly superior for patients and practitioners—and, in our industry, that comes from having what I like to call content confidence.

We also incorporated the idea of the irresistibly superior product into our transformation journey. We modernized our technology. We upgraded our content, reexamining it through the lens of health equity and diversity issues. And we had our content reviewed, validated, and certified by POCMA. This helps ensure that our content confidence translates to our partners. When we thought about how to take Jon R. Moeller's idea of irresistible superiority and bake it into the point-of-care marketing industry (which is very different from selling soap in stores), we realized that building content confidence was the answer.

That's why we've so actively embraced POCMA from a verification and auditing perspective. If a client is paying for a million patient guides, we want them to have total confidence that they are getting exactly a million patient guides. If they're paying for two thousand digital screens, we want them to have total confidence that they are getting two thousand digital screens. That level of validation, verification, and authenticity—on top of the rigorous process that goes into creating the content itself—helps to maintain that content confidence. And that's how we can be sure that we have our own irresistibly superior products.

Get Obsessed with Your Customer

High-level transformation requires changes not only internally but also externally, in the greater world, beyond company walls—the world where your customers, clients, and target audiences are impacted. This is a hurdle many companies have trouble overcoming when enacting change: cohesively carrying through a transformation behind closed doors *and beyond* so that changes on the inside actually reach the people who matter the most on the outside, the consumer.

How can you make sure your internal changes are also translated externally? What can you do to make sure the changes you implement behind the scenes, so to speak, also benefit the people on the outside—your customers, clients, or target audience? And how are those intersections between internal and external evolution crystallized, seen not only in words or ideas but also in action?

One tip I've found effective in my career when it comes to ensuring that internal and external transformation run in parallel—or, better yet, becomes entwined into a single transformation journey—is to take a customer-centric approach from the start. Part of that comes from developing the irresistibly superior product, as described earlier. Developing that kind of product requires being well attuned to the customers' needs and wants. After all, they are the judge of what is or isn't irresistibly superior.

But it's not just a question of product or service development. It's also a question of how you approach and interact with consumers. To put it bluntly, you've got to get obsessed with them; they should be the center of your (professional!) world.

This is an attitude I likely took away from my time with agencies: agencies are inherently client-focused businesses. The magic happens in front of the client. That's where the revenue comes from. So, in an agency setting, you can't just talk about a culture of customer centricity; you have to really live it.

In transformation, fostering this kind of customer-/client-focused culture requires the action of the storyteller-in-chief. That individual should be willing to demonstrate a customer-/client-first commitment through actions, not just words. This becomes even more critical when you're dealing with external audiences. You can't just tell a client, "Hey, *you* come first! We're here to make *you* happy!" because that's what any company is going to say. You've got to clearly communicate that value and then you've got to live it, demonstrably, every day in every interaction, big or small.

I personally believe in being a living example as a storyteller-in-chief. This is especially true when it comes to creating that culture of customer/client obsession. If you were to open my calendar when I'm heading up an agency, for example, you'd see that I meet clients three days a week—sometimes more. I think that boots-on-the-ground approach is communicating something to both the clients and the teams internally, attesting to Health Monitor's core values of teamwork, initiative, and transparency.

It's not just the CEO at the top saying, "We need to be more customer centric." The CEO is *living* this idea of customer centricity. It's one thing to say it in a video. It's one thing to write it in a memo. But it's another thing altogether to see the CEO personally make that commitment to a customer with a face-to-face meeting. I want my teams to know, "Hey, I'm out there with you. I'm facing a happy customer. I'm facing an unhappy customer. What's more, if you've got an unhappy customer, that's the first place I want to go. Let me get my hands dirty." It's all about reinforcing a commitment to a customer-centric ethos, at every level.

This kind of consistency and authenticity is key. If there's anything amiss, if what you preach versus what you practice isn't matching up, the friction point becomes very obvious very quickly. And you've got to anticipate a tougher audience with your external stakeholders compared to your internal stakeholders—because your clients will call you out pretty fast if they sense any hypocrisy in what you're saying versus what you're doing.

Say I'm telling my clients a story about how the company has pivoted to become focused on the digital future. I'm telling them all about how we're launching more digital products and expanding our digital footprint. I'm telling them about the cutting-edge new tech we're implementing, touting all these new developments. But then I show up to a client meeting taking notes with an old-fashioned notepad and paper. It's a record scratch moment, right? My words and my actions aren't aligning. That's an inconsistency clients will pick up on.

You have to live the brand in every aspect. If you're with a digital communications agency, you want your client presentations to be cutting edge. If you're in sales, you want to use modern customer relationship management software to keep up with your contacts. Your employees also need to live the brand: if your company prides itself on being agile and fast moving, you need people who are nimble and able to pivot quickly. If an employee tells a client, "Hey, I'll have that product for you by X date," then they better deliver that product by X date.

The great brands out there demonstrate this kind of consistency really well. A brand like Mercedes-Benz makes buying and owning a luxury car an *experience*. Even after you bring the car home from the dealership, if you have to take it to get serviced, you'll see the luxury ideal upheld. The service area might be an elegant waiting room, where somebody is serving you a cup of Italian espresso in fine china. It's all about consistency. They don't just *tell* you they're a luxury car brand. They're showing you, at every step, that it is.

That's what you've got to do as a storyteller-in-chief. You can't really deliver the sermons about your new values and your transformation journey to your clients in the way that you can to your internal teams. However, you can *show* your clients how changes are being made, through your interactions, through your processes, and through your revamped products. By embodying the change in front of clients, by showing them tangible results, you can reinforce the organization's transformation with great authenticity.

In Health Monitor's case, that means placing a premium on our relationships with our customers, the pharmaceutical and medical device companies, and their ad and media agencies. However, it also means nurturing the relationships with the end users of our products, the target audience of our content—physicians and patients. We're very cognizant of the need to foster that customer-centric culture in this context too. In this case, we might call it audience centric, since we aren't charging the physicians or patients for our services or products—they're simply the end users.

We know that we have to cater to these end users at every step. That's why Health Monitor is so dedicated to gathering data on how our products are used. That's why we have teams that visit physicians' offices, making sure the tech is working and getting feedback on how it could be improved. That audience-centric approach is how we can make sure that our products remain relevant, on point—and irresistibly superior.

Be Open to Constant Change

I've mentioned a few times already that transformation is a constant process. That kind of perpetual evolution is also critical to maintaining competitive advantage. Companies that embrace constant change will manage to stay at the front of the pack. I think great companies never stop transforming. That's why the landscape of what we considered great companies twenty-five years ago isn't the same as the landscape of great companies we champion today. There are names that endure and that we still talk about: Coca-Cola, P&G, Mercedes. And there are names that we talk about less often or not at all: Kodak, Blackberry, Oldsmobile.

It's not a question of luck. The companies that make it are making it in very challenging markets. The car industry is an interesting case study right now. We've got Elon Musk bringing the Tesla to market. Meanwhile, on the consumer side, we've got a broad interest in minimizing the use of fossil fuels. How are other manufacturers responding? Mercedes has the EQ range. Audi has their e-tron vehicles. Ford has even taken the iconic Mustang and developed the Mustang Mach-E.

These companies don't stick to what they've always done. They recognize that the world is changing and that the market is changing and that they need to change with it. Maintaining a competitive edge means being open to that kind of ongoing evolution. Companies that fail on that point are bound to get stuck in a rut.

It's a little bit like people who think their education ends as soon as they're handed a diploma. It comes down to that fixed versus growth mindset idea that psychologists throw at people. Someone with a growth mindset will look at a hurdle or setback and think to themselves, "Okay, how do I do better next time? What can I learn from this? What do I take away from this?" Someone with a fixed mindset is just going to run into the hurdle and see it as a stopping point. They won't use it to learn and then to carry on, more likely to succeed thanks to their newfound knowledge.

Constant learning is how we transform, as individuals and as companies. I think that constant learning and the personal transformation it brings makes people better employees. It makes people better spouses. It makes people *better* in general. When we restrict ourselves to fixed and rigid mindsets, that's where the danger lies. That's when we are likely to get stuck and stagnate, mired in the bog.

Constant learning is how we transform, as individuals and as companies.

My education hasn't ended. My formal education in the classroom has. But I learn things every day. I learn things every week. I will always be a ship at sea; I will never be a ship at port. That's a motto of mine that I adhere to in both my personal and my professional lives. I refuse to stop and drop anchor and say, "Okay, I'm done. Boy, I don't want to learn anything anymore, and I don't want to meet anybody new. I don't want to try anything new. I think I'm just going to sit." That works for me on vacation for about three days and then I'm like, "Okay, I've read the book. I sat on the beach. Where are we going next?"

I think great companies never stop learning, from both their success stories and their mistakes. That's what lets a company remain relevant in the future in a world where it's increasingly easy to become irrelevant. Transformation is never done. It's constant. It's best captured with a visual of a circle made up of constant arrows in a loop, as opposed to the left to right, A to B arrow that implies a set finishing point, a definitive conclusion.

The Health Monitor story is a prime example of that fact. The company never resigned itself to stagnancy. We had a long history of creating these wonderful print patient guides for physician waiting rooms. Those then evolved into the placement of digital screens in physician exam rooms. And that's led to other innovations, like giving patients the opportunity to access information on their mobile phones (for example, via an app they download with a QR code).

In the future, there will be more changes. We are still a content-first company. We will always maintain a high commitment to quality content. But we will also look at ways to adapt that content—for example, to broader audiences or to new technologies. There are many other ways we might distribute that content in a value-added way in the future, ways that we may not even be able to imagine yet.

By being open to new media and willing to try out different formats, Health Monitor (and point-of-care organizations at large) can also create more potential touch points, more ways to reach patients. Again, there will always be people who want print products, which is wonderful. But there are also going to be people who want to watch a short-form video, for example. And maybe they don't want to watch that video just once: they may want to view it multiple times.

Take someone with a chronic illness like diabetes, for instance. They need to be educated not only about the medication they take but also about their diet and exercise—as well as possible comorbidities that relate to their illness. For example, diabetics are at risk of peripheral neuropathy. A small injury, like a blister, can heal slowly, causing ulcers or serious infections. This makes more attentive foot and skin care essential to overall well-being.

Someone with diabetes thus needs access to different kinds of information on an ongoing basis. With this kind of patient, there are many opportunities for multiple touch points over an extended period. Point-of-care marketing providers like Health Monitor—those with the content confidence I've discussed—can continue to add value to those patients' lives through diverse media, both in the doctor's office and beyond.

I see it as an opportunity to walk with the patient on their journey, in a way. Especially with tablets and mobile technology, patients can access information of all kinds and have that information at their fingertips at all times, literally. They can watch videos, take online quizzes, download apps, and more. Such technologies create the opportunity for continual engagement with patients.

At Health Monitor, we want to be cognizant of that potential. That's why we remain open to continually evolving our product offering, both in terms of content and technology. And I trust that embracing continual evolution in that way will reap rewards, as it already has. I believe that kind of openness to change is a must for any company hoping to stand the test of time and maintain a competitive advantage in the long term.

Maintaining a Competitive Advantage: The Point-of-Care Marketing Industry as an Example

The point-of-care marketing industry offers a compelling example of how competitive advantage can be maintained through openness to constant transformation. ZS Associates has great research on the utilization and growth of the point-of-care industry. They're an Evanston-based pharmaceutical industry strategy consulting boutique founded by two Kellogg School of Management (Northwestern University) professors, Andris Zoltners and Prabhakant (Prabha) Sinha, in 1983.[15]

ZS is highly respected by the pharmaceutical industry and has a strong track record of research. When it comes to the point-of-care industry, they've published data from both the pre- and the post-COVID-19 eras. Prepandemic research showed strong growth. For example, point-of-care investments grew from $400 million in 2014 to $440 million in 2015. ZS further projected growth at an accelerated rate of 15 percent CAGR from 2017 through 2020.[16] And then, of course, COVID-19 happened.

ZS presented their findings on the pandemic's impact on the point-of-care industry—and how it's rebounded since—at the POCMA Point of Care Summit in March 2022.[17] Like most industries, point-of-care experienced setbacks due to COVID-19. Point-of-care spending slowed in 2020, likely due to the pandemic. But, since then, thanks to increased demand, the industry has rebounded, reaching spending of more than $823 million in 2022, and that is forecasted to reach $1 billion.

A huge part of that rebound comes down to the point-of-care industry's willingness to evolve. For example, device and mobile are among the most promising channels, with high interest from media planners and buyers. Media companies can leverage device and mobile channels to stay technologically up to date—and to reach consumers

15 Kellogg School of Management, Northwestern University, "Andris A. Zoltners: ZS Associates," https://www.kellogg.northwestern.edu/faculty/zoltners/htm/zsassoci-ates.html.

16 Hensley Evans and Victoria Summers, "The Evolution of Point-of-Care Marketing in Pharma."

17 Victoria Summers, "POC Advertising: State of the Industry," presentation given at the 2022 Point of Care NowEvolution, New York, March 30, 2022.

who are spending more time on devices—for example, by browsing social media.

The industry is evolving in other ways too. The majority of point-of-care advertising targets consumers, which constitutes about 90 percent of point-of-care spending. Growth rates in consumer point-of-care are anticipated to outpace healthcare practitioner growth rates in 2023. This speaks to the increased spending by pharmaceutical companies in the point-of-care space: pharmaceutical clients usually focus on consumer-targeted campaigns while medical technology clients usually focus on healthcare-practitioner-targeted campaigns.

The pandemic was a headwind for the point-of-care industry. However, it ultimately resulted in only a temporary setback. Media planners across healthcare advertising still look to point-of-care media, especially for products in launch and growth phases. That continued value is largely thanks to the point-of-care industry's proven ability to pivot. Since the COVID-19 setback, the industry has come roaring back and continues to see double-digit growth—a normal rate of about 15 percent for the year. And future macro trends promise to make point-of-care advertising even more valuable going forward.

Macro Trends Impacting the Point-of-Care Industry's Future Competitiveness

Certain projected macro trends make point-of-care a great area for brands and advertisers to focus spending on. One is the ongoing aging of the population and the continued trends around healthcare utilization. For one thing, we're going to continue to see more and more people in more and more doctors' offices. According to WHO, from 2015 to 2050, the proportion of the global population that's over age sixty will grow from 12 percent to 22 percent, nearly doubling.[18]

This means we'll be seeing more people with age-related illnesses, including chronic conditions. These elderly populations also tend to have more comorbidities, requiring the management of multiple ailments concurrently. What we're seeing is an increased demand for healthcare, which corresponds to more people using healthcare systems—and more people demanding healthcare information.

The second key trend that is shaping the future of the point-of-care industry is largely related to COVID-19. Some people have called it the death of the pharma sales rep.[19] That language is likely more than a little exaggerated, but it does point to a noticeable trend. Following the move to virtual meetings during the pandemic, some big names in the business started to question the need for boots-on-the-ground sales reps. Major names like Pfizer and Amgen have already announced their plans to cut down on sales reps as meetings with healthcare practitioners largely become virtual.[20, 21]

These pharmaceutical manufacturers are learning that there are alternatives to having ever-larger (read: costly) in-person field forces. I'm not going to prognosticate on the future of the pharma sales rep, because that's not my aim, nor do I have the expertise to do so. But

18   World Health Organization, "Ageing and Health Fact Sheet," October 1, 2021, https://www.who.int/news-room/fact-sheets/detail/ageing-and-health.

19   Robin Robinson, "Where Have All the Sales Reps Gone?" Pharma Voice, January 1, 2015, https://www.pharmavoice.com/news/sales-reps-gone/613270/.

20   Michael Erman, "Exclusive: Pfizer to Cut U.S. Sales Staff as Meetings with Healthcare Providers Move to Virtual," Reuters, January 11, 2022, https://www.reuters.com/business/healthcare-pharmaceuticals/exclusive-pfizer-cut-us-sales-staff-meetings-move-virtual-2022-01-11/.

21   Beth Snyder Bulik, "Amgen Cuts 500 U.S. Jobs, Primarily Sales Reps, as COVID-19 Speeds a Shift to Digital," Fierce Pharma, February 3, 2021, https://www.fiercepharma.com/marketing/amgen-cuts-several-hundred-u-s-jobs-primarily-sales-reps-as-covid-19-speeds-a-shift-to.

these trends indicate a clear shift in the industry: pharma manufacturers have realized that, even though there are more physicians treating more patients, those physicians are looking to get information about products, brands, and clinical studies in a different way—a way that doesn't necessarily require an in-person meeting with a sales rep.

Point-of-care marketing is one solution. The industry is uniquely positioned at this time, as these two macro trends converge—more people getting older and needing more healthcare and fewer pharmaceutical reps going to doctors' offices. Point-of-care already has a foothold in the doctor's office. In Health Monitor's case, we've got a foot not only in the waiting room but also in the doctor's exam room. That's a very unique and promising position to be in, especially for those companies that commit to that content confidence I've mentioned previously.

At its core, point-of-care messaging is about educating people. At a time when more people are seeking health information, and when there is less direct face-to-face contact with pharmaceutical companies in the doctor's office, point-of-care products are well positioned to fill the gap. If you're a brand marketer, this is a chance to say, "Here's an opportunity to insert my educational message and my brand story *at the point of care*, in a way that can help shape a conversation between a patient and a physician."

A point-of-care product is a last-mile solution, which is why it's so powerful—especially in light of those larger macro trends I've mentioned. In consumer-packaged goods, the marketing on the shelf at the store can get a consumer to choose shampoo X over shampoo Y. Point-of-care marketing can have the same impact. Of course, that power needs to be handled with responsibility and awareness—which is why I'm so insistent on values and transparency, something I'll get into greater detail on in the next chapter.

Competitive Advantage:
It's Not about You

When companies think about maintaining a competitive advantage, the mindset can be very self-serving. How do we get ahead? How do we beat the competition? How do we win the race? How do we make the most money, attract the most consumers, win the most prizes? Guess what? That mindset isn't going to get you far. Companies that want to create a competitive edge in transformation need to be clear on one thing: it's not about them. The same is true for the storyteller-in-chief—it's not about you.

I think effectively creating a competitive advantage comes from looking outside—to your customer. You've got to create that irresistibly superior product that will win their heart and mind. And you've got accept the fact that the irresistibly superior product won't look the same from one year to the next. You have to keep evolving.

If you're P&G, you have to keep sending your team of scientists to your testing facility with all of its dishwashers. They've got to keep making those batches of mac and cheese so that they can keep testing out the latest dishwasher tablets. This all has to be done with the end consumer's needs and wants in mind. What will serve *them* best?

In Health Monitor's case, we have to keep in mind that the physicians we serve are evolving. Our products are used in the offices of healthcare professionals, and today's healthcare professionals are changing in many ways. First, they're more digitally fluent than they have been in the past. Doctors' offices are thus becoming more technologically advanced—for example, with the incorporation of electronic health records (EHR) instead of paper files to organize patient data.

The structure of physicians' workplaces is also changing. In the past, you had more doctors with individual practices, for example.

Now physicians are increasingly practicing in either health systems or larger group practices.

Doctors themselves are changing too. We are lucky to work with a much more diverse group of healthcare professionals than in the past. The average physician in 1980 was predominantly a white male. Today, more women than men are enrolled in medical school, according to data from the Association of American Medical Colleges.[22] This data also shows that medical schools are becoming increasingly ethnically and racially diverse. In 2021, Black or African American students comprised 11.3 percent of matriculants, up from 9.5 percent in 2020. The number of students of Hispanic, Latino, and Spanish origin likewise increased, comprising 12.7 percent of matriculants in 2021, up from 12 percent in 2020.[23]

Health Monitor is cognizant of the ways that physicians' offices and physicians themselves are evolving. We know that it's on us to adapt accordingly, considering everything from our product offering to how we approach physicians' offices. By acknowledging the reality of the new practice setting—from the new physician to the new technologies—we're able to keep our competitive advantage. Those things impact our business and force us to keep innovating, for the better.

This attitude is one that Health Monitor and the point-of-care industry at large has embraced, and that's why I have such high hopes for both. I don't think we'll be going the way of the Oldsmobile. I think we'll continue to evolve, adapt to new contexts, and adopt new technologies—all in the name of better serving healthcare profession-

---

22 Patrick Boyle, "More Women Than Men Are Enrolled in Medical School," AAMC News, December 9, 2019, https://www.aamc.org/news-insights/ more-women-men-are-enrolled-medical-school.

23 Stuart Heiser, "Medical School Enrollment More Diverse in 2021," AAMC, December 8, 2021, https://www.aamc.org/news-insights/press-releases/ medical-school-enrollment-more-diverse-2021.

als and their patients. And it's precisely *because* we take that mindset that we will be permitted to continue thriving.

You Won't Get Your Competitive Advantage without the First Two Cs

This chapter has been all about maintaining that competitive advantage—the thing that lets you do better than the proverbial other guy. Competitive edge is a crucial consideration when you're entering a transformation journey. The last thing you want to do is enact changes that will result in a company *losing* its marketplace advantage, right? Ideally, you're hoping to implement changes that will improve that advantage.

> **Competitive advantage can't be the entire driver for change. It can't be the sole focus.**

But here's the thing: competitive advantage can't be the entire driver for change. It can't be the sole focus. You've still got to address those other components of culture and communication. If you don't address all three Cs, you aren't ready to run the race of the transformation journey. It would be like trying to win the race with one shoe on: painful, damaging, and definitely not going to result in a winning finishing time.

The good news is that when you align those first pieces of the puzzle, the culture and communication pieces, the third piece tends to fall into place. When you build and communicate a values-based culture that keeps people engaged and motivated, you're going to have an easier time attracting great talent. That great talent is going to play a key role in getting that irresistibly superior product that you want developed, fine-tuned, produced, and sent out to the customer.

And once you have that irresistibly superior product, don't stop. If the product development team launches a product, they're entitled to order a sheet cake from Costco and throw some balloons and confetti around. But the very next day, you've got to sweep up the confetti and get back to work on the next thing. Because you're never done. You're never done innovating and staying ahead of change—not if you want to maintain that competitive edge.

You've got to keep innovating. Keep questioning what could be done better. Look to your consumers for the answer. They'll tell you. That's immensely valuable. Because, at the end of the day, your consumers are the people who will grant you a competitive advantage. But they can just as well rescind that advantage if they aren't happy with what you're offering.

So when you're thinking about that competitive advantage, remember: it's not about you. It's about meeting the needs of consumers, your audience. By focusing on their needs, you'll be able to create the products and services they want and be able to build that loyal following that leads to longevity in the marketplace. Focusing on genuinely meeting your target audience's needs—not profits or sales or catchy ads—is good business sense. From an ethical standpoint, it's also the *right thing to do*.

In my view, that's an idea that isn't discussed often enough in the business world: doing the right thing. In any board meeting, you're more likely to hear discussions about profits and products than ethics. Unfortunately, ignoring ethics can lead to missteps—missteps that hurt companies and, more profoundly, the consumers they're supposed to cater to. That's why I place such a premium on values and transparency, especially in pivotal transformation journeys—and that's why I've dedicated the entire final section of this book to that conversation.

PART 3

TRANSFORMING THE INDUSTRY

CHAPTER 6

VALUES AND TRANSPARENCY

Every industry has its scandals now and again, and ours is no exception. The point-of-care marketing industry had its moment of reckoning in 2018. At that time, a competitor—one that's no longer in the industry—was brought to task and accused of not having accurately delivered on the promised media placement numbers. The incident was very public. It also resulted in the highly broadcasted removal of the CEO of that organization.

Further, that incident had an impact on the industry as a whole, with other organizations being brought under the microscope or called into question. It created quite the hurricane, and that hurricane left some destruction in its path. However, like everything in life, there was a positive side to that hurricane. It tore down some of the bad—and it encouraged rebuilding of the good.

In response to that incident, the firms that remain in the industry today stepped forward to find a solution. That solution was working with POCMA to develop and ratify the validation and verification standards for media numbers that we all use today. Under this system, any advertising agency or marketer that is utilizing point-of-care media can be assured that the reporting, verification, auditing, and certification of those audits is rigorous and reliable.

The audits are done by third parties, assuring total confidence in the system. As noted earlier in the book, at Health Monitor, we've had our entire platform certified. That certification doesn't apply only to an individual campaign. The entire platform has been certified for its veracity, authenticity, and reliability, for both print and digital, by an independent third-party group. It's a milestone I'm immensely proud of.

That 2018 hurricane rocked the point-of-care marketing industry. But I think we proved that we could pivot, and we could come back better. That was the first strong headwind the point-of-care marketing industry faced. The second was the COVID-19 pandemic; in the previous chapter, I discussed how the industry has managed, also in that instance, to pivot and come back stronger.

My point is this: transformation is often born of facing headwinds. And in those instances, it's always important to come back to the north point on the compass, the trajectory you've set out for yourself. And that trajectory needs to be guided by values and transparency. In the previous chapters, I've laid out the core principles that, in my experience, are necessary for successful transformation: culture, communication, and competitive advantage. There's one last point I want to address now, which is important to any successful organization—values and transparency.

Strong, solid values are critical to weathering any tough storm. Without them, you lose the north point on your compass—and have a good chance of getting lost at sea. With this final chapter, I want to talk about the importance of values. Believe me, they matter. They matter not only from an ethical perspective but also from a business perspective, because good values and ethical behavior benefit all involved.

Ethics Are Nonnegotiable (Period)

Strong values come from good ethics. And, in my view, ethics are nonnegotiable. I don't want to get into some philosophical debate on the nature of ethics and ethical behavior (I'd rather watch *Hamilton* than read Socrates or Plato, to be honest). When talking about ethical behavior, I like to ask myself: *Is it the right thing to do?* It's that simple.

We all know what the "right" thing to do is, even when we don't want to admit it. Sometimes it's the harder option. But I believe that humans, generally, have an ingrained sense of wrong and right, a biologically set north point on the compass. We just need to make sure we follow it.

I remember when I was preparing for my father's funeral. I asked my son to help me polish his shoes, the ones he would wear in the casket. My son, a middle-schooler at the time, asked me, "Hey, Dad, why are we doing this? Nobody is going to see these shoes anyway."

It was a fair question. And I only had one answer for him: "Because it's the right thing to do." There was nothing else to it, in my mind. I wanted to give my dad a final show of respect, and polishing his shoes was part of that. It was just the right thing to do.

In personal or professional life, strong values and good ethics are not negotiable, in my opinion. If you're going to be a change agent, a storyteller-in-chief, if you're going to enact transformation, you can't neglect these points. You also can't just give them lip service. You have to not only speak but also live your values, day in and day out. And for organizations at large to succeed, everybody needs to stick to those values and uphold good ethics.

I like to say that a lot of life is gray, but ethical matters are black and white. This is a guiding light that I've followed throughout my career, and it's helped with many tough decisions. For example, over the course of my career, I've seen plenty of situations where a high-performing individual gets great results—but is then revealed to adhere to ethically dubious practices. As a leader, what do you do in these cases?

> **I like to say that a lot of life is gray, but ethical matters are black and white.**

Say you've got a great field sales representative and they're turning out excellent numbers, getting fantastic results on the page. But, all of a sudden, something comes to light about that person's behavior. Maybe they've crossed professional boundaries or made underhanded deals or acted otherwise unprofessionally. We're talking about what they do Monday through Friday, from nine to five; in that context, some line has been crossed.

Of course it needs to be addressed. You can't ignore it. You can't say, "Hey, but this person is turning out great numbers," and sweep it under the rug. I mean, you can try, but it's very likely going to come back to haunt you. In my view, you've got to address these moments head-on—and the sooner, the better.

I've had plenty of these moments over the course of my career, where we get the senior manager of the department and the head of HR and myself in a conference room to talk about this kind of a situation. We have to sit there and say, "Well, what do we do about this individual and their behavior?" The behavior in question varies from one case to the next. Usually, it's that they've acted in a way that is inappropriate or that goes against our values as a business.

Those discussions aren't fun. When you're having them, you're making a choice that impacts a person's life and livelihood. But I've also never found those discussions very difficult, because I've always taken a hard line on ethics, both personally and professionally. Again, a lot of life is gray, but ethical matters are black and white.

As a result, I've always chosen to terminate the employee. That's the right thing to do, in my view. This can be a topic of debate. Other people might say, "Well, let's just give them a slap on the wrist, because they're getting such good numbers, and we wouldn't want to not have that sales territory filled." To me, those are dangerous compromises to make.

When you don't terminate someone who has exhibited poor ethical behavior, you invariably end up making compromises. And I think you're then headed down a very slippery slope, both as a leader and as an organization. Especially in organizations where the transgressions of senior leaders are visible, this creates a huge problem. The rest of the organization sees a signal about whether certain behaviors are tolerated. If they see that unethical behaviors are permitted, that can create a situation where those unethical behaviors are normalized and, as a result, spread more widely.

In my view, it's better to just make the cut. If an employee is not following the proverbial ethical north point, I have no qualms about letting them go. In each of those instances where I've had to make that kind of cut, if I had to do it over, I'd do it the same way again. Whether it's a business situation or your personal life, there have to be some boundaries that are indisputable—boundaries that are truly hard and fast, black and white. And I think it's the ethical ones that deserve that designation.

Values and Transparency Benefit All Involved

One reason I place such a premium on ethics is that ethics build trust, and trust is where all good relationships begin, both professional and personal. Plus, trust is good for business. You want your employees to trust you. You want your clients to trust you. You want your customers to trust you. You want the public to trust you. All of that adds up to a stronger, more resilient business.

There's plenty of evidence to that fact—it's not just me proselytizing. The pharmaceutical industry is an excellent example of how trust can benefit all involved. Take clinical trials, for example. Clinical trials are used by pharmaceutical companies to test out new drugs. This is an incredibly in-depth and rigorous process, with multiple phases, starting with preclinical or laboratory studies all the way up to testing on humans (this is a much later stage in the process and only comes after rigorous testing for a new molecule's efficacy and safety first).

In the past, there wasn't a great deal of transparency around clinical trials. It's taken decades, but that's changed. In 1997, Congress passed the Food and Drug Administration Modernization Act (FDAMA), requiring all clinical trials to be registered.[24] Afterward, the National Institutes of Health (NIH) was required to create a public information resource on trials. In 2000, the website ClinicalTrials.gov was estab-

24   ClinicalTrials.gov, "History, Policies, and Laws," https://clinicaltrials.gov/ct2/about-site/history.

lished. This was a publicly accessible database of clinical trials, mostly those funded by the NIH. In 2008, ClinicalTrials.gov began allowing the submission of clinical studies results. As of September 2009, the submission of adverse event information became mandatory.

This is just a handful of legislative and administrative steps that have been taken in the past decades to increase transparency around clinical trials. I could go on. But the point is this: if you're putting medicines on the market, medicines that impact everyday people, isn't it logical that those people have a chance to understand how those medicines are made? To know what adverse side effects they might experience from taking them? To know what organizations funded their development? Transparency around clinical trials seems like the right thing to do, in my view.

Such transparency has benefits. It builds trust between consumers and the pharmaceutical industry, for one. It also helps create a more inclusive healthcare field. For example, one piece of clinical trials policy relates to the inclusion of women and minorities as participants in research involving human subjects. This is critical to ensuring that research findings are applicable to the *entire* population. The same statute also requires clinical trials be designed to provide information about discrepancies according to sex, gender, race, or ethnicity.[25]

The Physician Payments Sunshine Act (PPSA), often referred to simply as the Sunshine Act, is another great example from the pharmaceutical industry of the benefits of transparency. It requires drug and device manufacturers to collect data on gifts and payments made to teaching hospitals and physicians. The companies must keep an open registry of any honorary payments made to physicians, whether

---

25   NIH, Grants and Funding, "Inclusion of Women and Minorities as Participants in Research Involving Human Subjects," https://grants.nih.gov/policy/inclusion/women-and-minorities.htm.

it's for speaking, advising, consulting—whatever the case may be. Until the Sunshine Act, many physicians were making hundreds of thousands of dollars in consulting and speaking fees.

The Sunshine Act intended to, as the name suggests, throw a little light on the situation. Light can also be used to disinfect and cleanse. And that's exactly what that piece of legislation accomplished. It helped to get rid of those cases of unwarranted, overstuffed payments. It helped to make sure that any fees were legitimately earned and in no way perceived as a quid pro quo for prescribing behavior. It was another necessary step toward transparency for Big Pharma, an industry that had been historically shrouded in secrecy.

I think these changes have made the industry better. It's helped to build trust through tangible actions, not just words. Trust has to be earned. It has to be built. You can't just tell someone, "Hey, trust me!" You've got to show that you're trustworthy. It's the same way that you can't tell someone, "Hey, I'm funny!" Well, tell me a joke then—and it better be a good one.

When it comes to trust, people need proof. I think we live in a time where there is healthy skepticism toward authority and authority figures, whether that's an individual or an organization. That has helped create this call for more "Show me, don't tell me," especially when it comes to demonstrating trustworthiness. And I think that's a good thing.

Greater transparency can also help build greater trust in organizations, regardless of the field. If a company and its leadership just *do the right thing*, employees will recognize that. Clients will recognize that. Partners will recognize that. And doing the right thing comes down to many of the points I've touched on in previous chapters: eliminating cocktail napkin deals, knocking down silos, and getting rid of superficial signs of hierarchy, like numbered parking spaces, to name just a few. Such acts demonstrate solid values and transparency, helping to create an organization that's trustworthy—an organization that people recognize does the right thing.

The Role of Values and Transparency in Improving Health Equity

I've spoken about the three Cs needed to achieve change—culture, communication, and competitive advantage. Values and transparency are the foundation upon which those three Cs are built. Looking ahead, I think, if more of us continue to rely on that foundation, we'll all enjoy a brighter, better future. This is especially true in the healthcare field.

I've touched on disparities in healthcare—for example, how the COVID-19 pandemic illuminated existing disparities. To reiterate, data from the CDC showed that Black or African American people were 2.9 times more likely than non-Hispanic white people to be hospitalized and 1.9 times more likely to die from COVID-19 infection. Meanwhile, Hispanic and Latino people were 3.1 times more likely than non-Hispanic white people to be hospitalized and 2.3 times more likely to die from COVID-19 infection. American Indian and Alaska Native people were 3.7 times more likely than non-Hispanic white people to be hospitalized and 2.4 times more likely to die from COVID-19 infection.[26]

Those are sobering figures. But it's important that they are brought to light. Again, I hate to credit the black-hatted villain of the play, COVID-19, with having done any good. But it's important to unmask these harsh truths about health inequity in

---

26   Centers for Disease Control and Prevention, "The Unequal Toll of the COVID-19 Pandemic."

our society—especially because, as I've noted, these issues go well beyond COVID-19.

The healthcare industry is big on quantitative numbers. Physicians can talk to you about your body mass index or your A1C, your glucose level, or your weight. Cholesterol numbers are big—maybe your doctor is always reminding you to bring those down. Point being, there are a lot of numbers that physicians look at to determine your health.

But, interestingly, the number in the US that best predicts your health outcomes is your zip code.[27] Now this is a huge, complex equation. There are many factors at play here, as a person's zip code can relate to things like socioeconomic status, education access, food access, and more. But one of them is undoubtedly healthcare access.

Disparities in healthcare access based on where a person lives (which often connects to socioeconomic status) is a huge issue. It's an issue we all have a responsibility to acknowledge and, if it's in our power to do so, to address. That applies whether you're a healthcare provider, a pharmaceutical company, or an advertising media firm like Health Monitor. We're all in this big basket together of delivering healthcare to patients in some way, all playing our part.

I think that this issue—of health equity and fairness—is a big, complex problem that requires a big, complex solution. It's a solution that we all have a role in creating. That includes companies like Health Monitor and people like me. As I've said, I recognize that the Nobel Committee is not going to come knocking on my door for what we do at Health Monitor. We have a very small part to play. But we do have our part to play. And I'm committed to that.

---

27   Jamie Ducharme and Elijah Wolfson, "Your Zip Code Might Determine How Long You Live—and the Difference Could Be Decades," *TIME*, June 17, 2019, https://time.com/5608268/zip-code-health/.

That's why we've done things like expand our Medical Advisory Board to include individuals with strong backgrounds in health equity. That's why we've committed to making sure we deliver our communications in the right language and through the right lens for different groups in different geographies. That's why we've invested in health communications literacy research that enables us to improve the clarity of our content. That's why we've made sure our products get distributed in underserved geographies. We believe in taking those steps because it's the right thing to do.

Those are just a few small examples of how values and transparency can benefit populations more broadly—and, in the case of the healthcare industry, potentially improve health equity. Again, Health Monitor's part is small. But if everybody did their small part, think of what we might accomplish. And it all starts with that simple concept of ethics—doing something because it's the right thing to do.

A Commitment to Values and Transparency Starts with You, the Storyteller-in-Chief

I believe it's the storyteller-in-chief's job to set the tone when it comes to these cornerstones of change. I've talked about a few ways in which I've promoted certain values in my time at Health Monitor. I had the numbered parking spaces removed and got rid of the executive washroom in the interests of greater equality and less hierarchy. I promoted data sharing with our clients' agency partners in the interests of greater transparency. And I encouraged initiatives like the on-the-spot bonus system in the interests of greater positivity.

You can promote values and transparency as a storyteller-in-chief through your actions as well as through your words. However, you also need the people around you to promote those same values and act transparently. You'll only achieve the meaningful change you want if you get everyone sailing to the same north point on your compass, remember?

The problem is that, when you're the one in charge, you're often (ironically) left in the dark. If something goes wrong, people around you might try to fix it before reporting it to you—rather than reporting it to you right away. That approach can result in small problems becoming big problems. In the worst cases, small problems can become unfixable issues.

How can you avoid that nightmare scenario? You've got to make sure your people trust you, the storyteller-in-chief, with both the good *and* the bad. I always like a good story to drive my point home, and I pull out the cold cup of coffee anecdote when I'm conveying this to my team, when I want them to understand that "Hey, you really *can* tell me everything, even when things go wrong."

A US Navy admiral, when he was newly promoted, famously said he knew that his new status meant two things: first, that every time he stepped on a new ship, he would never be handed a cold cup of coffee again—and, second, that he would never hear the whole truth on a ship again. He felt that, as the authority figure, he wouldn't be shared the inner workings of the ship, especially if there were problems. People would try to fix things, to package them a certain way first, rather than tell him the harsh truth. He'd always get that piping hot cup of coffee. But he wouldn't hear about the fact that they'd almost burned down the galley making it.

So whenever I've entered a new role as a storyteller-in-chief, I've told that story. I've then told my team, "Unlike that particular admiral in his starched whites and his shoulder boards, I prefer my coffee cold." And I take practical steps to make sure that I'm delivered that cold cup of coffee, when necessary.

At Health Monitor, for example, in addition to a standing senior leadership team meeting every other week, I also have one-on-one meetings with each senior leader. The rubric for those meetings basically consists of three points. First, what's going on in your world that you want to make me aware of? Second, if you've got obstacles, what can I do to help? And third, what's the cold cup of coffee—what's the thing you don't want to tell me? What's the thing that's broken? What's the thing that's frustrating you?

As a storyteller-in-chief, you'll get greater transparency from your people if you tell them, "It's okay to serve me a cold cup of coffee." It's awesome when they've got their own thoughts on potential solutions. I always encourage people to try to think about solutions. But, candidly, a lot of times, the problem is something that's beyond their functional department.

This speaks to the point on breaking down silos I've made previously. Often, it's not a limitation on the individual's part that's kept them from solving a problem on their own; it's simply an issue that needs interdepartmental collaboration and, for that to happen, more senior leadership needs to get involved. That's okay. It's better to call more hands on deck than to have people stewing and fretting about a problem that *seems* unfixable—but simply needs additional support.

In my roles as a storyteller-in-chief, I always wanted to create a culture from the outset where it was perfectly okay to come in and say, "Hey, we're behind on this key project because we're lacking these resources." I wanted to create that ability to be transparent, even with bad news. I'll admit, I'm the kind of person who will ask for six things when I know it's only humanly possible to complete five of those six.

So I need to recognize that and empower people to say, "Hey, I can only get you five of the six."

Sometimes, as the storyteller-in-chief, you're going to get a cold cup of coffee. If you get that cold cup of coffee, you're on the right track toward meaningful transformation. You've done something right: you've created a culture of values and transparency, where people know it's okay to give you that cold cup of coffee. If you're always getting your coffee piping hot, everything is always great, and nothing is ever wrong? Then I'd start to question things. I'd rather get a cold cup of coffee on occasion than get a hot cup served to me every time.

> I'd rather get a cold cup of coffee on occasion than get a hot cup served to me every time.

Empowering Your People to Embrace Values and Transparency

Values and transparency are rooted in culture. I've said before that I think culture, from my experience, is the most important part of transformation. It's where the change journey starts and ends. Without strong cultural values guiding your ship, serving as the north point on your compass, you're unlikely to see a transformation journey through to the end. Because, as I've discussed, transformation is tough. Change is hard. Humans are creatures of habit. We don't like to change.

But change is often necessary. Sometimes it's thrust upon as—as happened with me in my personal life. Change can also be thrust upon organizations—as happened with Health Monitor and the COVID-19 pandemic. Change can also be thrust upon entire industries. That was the case with the point-of-care marketing industry, when it was rocked by a scandal surrounding a lack of transparency in 2018.

So what's the next step for you? As a storyteller-in-chief, how can you make strong ethics part of everyday action, not just thought? It all comes back to what I told my son when we were polishing my father's shoes ahead of his funeral: *it's the right thing to do*. I think just asking yourself that at every step—Is this the right thing to do?—is all you need to get started. Because, as I mentioned, I think humans have an innate sense of right and wrong. You know what the right thing to do is. So do it. Ha! Sound too simple?

My advice is this: put into place the policies and structures you need to make it easier to do the right thing. That's largely what this book has been about. Yes, it's been about enacting transformation at organizations. But here's my little secret: enacting change, creating a transformation, inciting a revolution (if you want to be dramatic) is all about *doing the right thing*. That's usually what we're looking for when we want a change. We want to do the right thing.

So put into place the policies that make it easier to do the right thing. Get rid of the cocktail napkin deals. Get rid of the meeting after the meeting. Get rid of the siloes. Add positive aspects that encourage action, like on-the-spot bonuses. And empower your people.

Empowering your people is one of the most important things you can do. As a storyteller-in-chief, I know that I have a role as an architect and a catalyst. But it works only if everyone is empowered. That requires the critical direct line of senior leaders that report to the chief executive, as well as everyone under them, feeling like they have an important part to play—and that they have the personal agency needed to play that part without micromanagement.

Again, I have a navy-related anecdote that helps drive this point home. I'm getting self-conscious about the number of naval anecdotes in this book (it's starting to make me look like a Naval Academy dropout, I think), so this is the last one. I promise.

During the Napoleonic Wars, there was the Battle of Trafalgar, which pitted the British against a combined French and Spanish armada. The traditional method of warfare on the high seas at the time was for the two sides—in this case the British versus the allied forces—to line up opposite one another, forming two parallel lines. And then they'd fire at each other.

On the British side, the commanders of the ship would be looking to the admiral's ship, the flagship, for their signals to determine when to fire, when to stop firing, and so on. And those signals were given via flags—hence the term *flagship*. Hey, they didn't have cell phones or radio technology back then. It worked. (As an aside, this is where our modern use of the term *flagship* comes from—like when people say they have their flagship store on Fifth Avenue.)

Before the Battle of Trafalgar, British Admiral Horatio Nelson gathered his commanders to go over their battle plans. And he told them, "We're not going to do it the usual way" (not a direct quote—I'm sure he was more eloquent). He pivoted. Instead of lining up opposite the allied ships to create two parallel lines, he wanted the British ships to go at the French and Spanish ships *perpendicularly*. This would then forcibly cut the allied line and scramble their boats. But the problem was, it would also scramble the British boats. If they weren't all in their usual line, there was a good chance that they wouldn't be able to see the admiral's flagship. How could they know what to do?

The admiral left that decision to his commanders. He gave them intellectual ownership of the decision. If they looked to the flagship and couldn't find it, he trusted them to act correctly. He basically told them to get alongside the enemy and fight according to their best judgment. And that became the Battle of Trafalgar. Nelson was outnumbered, with twenty-seven British ships up against thirty-three allied ships. In the resulting battle, the allies lost nineteen to twenty ships while the British lost none.[28]

So why am I subjecting you to one last naval anecdote? I think that story perfectly encapsulates how great companies function. You have admirals who trust and empower their commanders to do the right thing, to the best of their ability.

The CEO of a one-hundred-thousand-person firm is not on every production line, watching every razor blade or car or kid's toy come off the line. That CEO is not in every sales meeting with every customer. They're not in every warehouse, watching every box get packed. They're not in every presentation with the ad agency, making sure that the television spots are great. It physically and mentally wouldn't be possible.

It's all about building a great team and then really, truly empowering them and letting them know that they can take the initiative to act. And you've got to make that clear to your leadership team. Have that meeting where you say, "I'm not going to give you a signal from the flagship for every move. I trust you to make the move." And then encourage them to take the initiative—to make their department as great as it can be, make their product as great as it can be, make the environment for their people as productive and fun and growth oriented as it can be.

If you've taken the effort to create an ethical culture, one built on strong values and transparency, you'll be able to put that trust in your people. And they'll be able to trust you in return, to trust that you

---

28   Encyclopaedia Britannica, "Battle of Trafalgar," September 2, 2022, https://www. britannica.com/event/Battle-of-Trafalgar-European-history.

really *mean* it when you say you want them to take initiative—and that you won't punish them for taking that initiative (or, on a similar note, for serving up the occasional cold cup of coffee).

When you've set up that kind of structure and dynamic, change becomes easier. It becomes a "we" equation instead of a "me" equation, which is exactly how great change happens. Yes, as the storyteller-in-chief, you set the tone. You put into place policies and structures. But you don't go it alone. You empower people to join you on the journey and in the commitment to a more values-based, transparent culture.

Looking Ahead: Creating a Future Built on Values and Transparency

I've said before that change is a never-ending process. If you visualized it, it would be a circle of connected arrows—not one arrow pointing from A to B, left to right. The same is true for the foundations of change: you can't just plant your flag for values and transparency once, institute some policies, and call it a day. You have to continuously live your commitment to values and transparency. Part of that means finding new, innovative ways to live out those ethics that you've build your organization on and that have guided your transformational journey.

I've talked about how we embraced a more transparent approach at Health Monitor by sharing the details of our physician networks with advertising agency media departments. That was one of the first things we did when I joined. We approached those agency partners of our clients and told them, "Look, with the proper confidentiality documentation in place, we're happy to share this data with you. You can use it for your media planning." And that step has certainly borne fruit for us and improved our relationships with both our clients and their agency partners.

But we aren't done. We're constantly looking for more ways to improve transparency, to further promote our values. The continuation of that, the next step, is an industry advisory board, which we're now doing once a year. We invite senior people from the industry, both from advertising agencies and pharmaceutical companies, and we show them the latest innovations we're working on. That could mean new products, either print or digital, for example—or new means of data collection, so that we can get them feedback about their campaigns faster. Whatever we're working on, we share it with them during that annual industry advisory board event.

It's a lot like when a pharmaceutical company does an innovation day, where they have their head of R&D show people, "Here's what's in our development pipeline. Here are the new molecules that we're testing to see if they could be safe and efficacious in treating these disease areas. Here's what we're working on that may one day come to market." It's the same idea.

It's not a question of salesmanship. It's simply about providing the information so that they're aware of what opportunities are coming down the pipeline for them. It's also an opportunity for honest feedback. They can provide input and ask questions. And we get to have those discussions: "Hey, that's pretty cool. Could I pilot that? Could I test that? What if you did it slightly differently?"

I think that level of transparency is good for innovation and for partnerships. It's also going to result in the best products for the end consumers, our ultimate target audience: the physicians and their patients. Last but certainly not least: It's simply *the right thing to do*. And I firmly believe that long-term success is built on doing the right thing, on giving voice and action to values and transparency.

In chapter 3, I spoke about culture, the first point to address in a transformation journey, and I talked about finding that north point on your compass. You've got to stake out the cultural values you want to build your evolution on, and you've got to articulate (and act on) those values, with great consistency and clarity. You've got to do it all

There's one north point on the compass we should all keep in mind, and that's a commitment to values and transparency.

with your north point in mind—that destination of what direction you want to go in and where you want to end up.

Maybe your north point is to double your company's size. Maybe your north point is to triple your annual profits. Maybe your north point is to develop five new products in five months—or to win one million new subscribers in a year. Maybe your north point is simply to become a more agile, innovative company. Maybe it's just to regain a competitive edge that was lost, to avoid joining the Kodaks and the Oldsmobiles of the business world.

I don't know what your north point in your change journey is—it depends on the company and the industry you're in and on your organizational goals. You're the one who has to figure out the north point for your change journey. But there's one north point on the compass we should all keep in mind, and that's a commitment to values and transparency. It's a north point we can use not only in our professional but also in our private lives. And it's a north point that will serve us well if we adhere to it. It's one that benefits us all. It's the easiest one to articulate: it's just a matter of doing what's right.

THE GIFT OF THE PIVOT

When I look back on my career, I can see that the pivots were some of the most valuable moments for my development. They were critical to my long-term success. But, to be honest, I wasn't always happy about those pivots while they were happening. It's taken me years to recognize the gift of the pivot. My time at Roche, which I mentioned briefly in the introduction, is one of the best examples.

Earlier in my career, I worked in Roche's diagnostics division, on the marketing side. I had always been adamant that I wanted to be in marketing, not in sales. It started with P&G: when that P&G recruiter found me on campus at Hamilton College and told me he wanted to interview me, I immediately told him that I would do anything to work for P&G—but that I wanted to be in marketing, not sales. After flying out to interview with P&G in Cincinnati, I ended up on their marketing team.

My dad had been in sales, and I had seen what that life looked like. And, while I loved him, he was always away, on the road, constantly traveling. He had limited downtime to spend with his friends and family. When he wasn't on a plane or in a car, he was often exhausted from his life on the go. I had seen how tough sales could be on a person.

I admired and respected my dad. He was a man with great convictions and great courage—and I know that I will never do anything nearly as important as he did in his lifetime: he was in France on June 6, 1944, earning a Purple Heart that day, and is buried in the National Cemetery. I am proud to be like my dad in many ways. I share his grit and his stamina. But I was determined not to be like him in one way: I would *not* be in sales like him.

I stubbornly stuck to that marketing-only career track mindset for years. I made it to the role of marketing director at Roche when I was pulled aside for my annual review. You can imagine my excitement when they said, "Congratulations, we're going to take you to the next step!" I thought they were going to make me vice president of marketing (ah, the naivete of youth). As you can probably already guess, that's not what happened.

Instead, they told me, "We're going to send you to the West Coast to be the area sales director."

I almost fell out of my chair. I tried to argue: "No, I'm a marketing guy! I'm not a sales guy!" But they weren't having it.

The general manager told me, "Dave, you're going to be a general manager someday. You need to get more rounded experiences than just marketing, marketing, and more marketing. Trust me: go out to the West Coast and run part of the sales organization. You'll learn a lot. We've got a plan for you."

So I did it. I wasn't happy about it. I was (metaphorically!) kicking and screaming and pouting like an angry kid. I was the petulant child, throwing my toys out of the crib in protest. It felt like a lateral move at the time. I wasn't getting the linear progression, from marketing director to VP of marketing, that I'd envisioned. But I trusted my manager. So, reluctantly, I went to California.

I went to the West Coast for a year, ran the western area sales team, and then came back. At that point, they gave me the whole sales organization to run. It was an unbelievable opportunity: I got to restructure the entire sales organization—with the benefit of firsthand knowledge.

Throughout that process, I learned a ton. I had been running a marketing department of about twenty-five people. Now I was running a sales organization about ten times that size, managing people and teams spread across different cities and geographies. It was a huge learning experience. How do you manage your time? How do you manage your teams? How do you motivate your people? Managing a salesperson was a little different from managing a marketing person. And managing a salesperson in Idaho was different from managing a salesperson in Los Angeles. It was a steep learning curve.

When you manage a large organization with a lot of people, there were always people issues that need to be adjudicated, with professionalism and empathy (and, yes, sometimes with firmness). I found myself dealing with those people problems every week. And, interestingly, the really wild and woolly situations, those requiring the most delicacy, always seemed to happen at five o'clock on a Friday. I'd be in the car heading home and somebody would call to quit. Or I'd be at Blockbuster Video (remember those?) with my takeout pizza in hand, trying to figure out what movie to rent, and I'd get the call from HR saying, "We have to report that so-and-so did something that's against our company policies and values. And we're going to have to deal with this in a significant way come Monday morning."

In comparison, life in the marketing department had been pretty structured. It was more strictly a nine-to-five gig. I had gone to California kicking and screaming. However, once I was out there, I quickly realized that I was using muscles I hadn't used before. I was truly learning in terms of the way I managed my time, the way I engaged with people, and the way I approached the differences in people to find the best in them (and to get them to be even better).

My experience in sales at Roche unlocked a lot. It taught me functional skills and improved me as a professional in many ways, from making me a better manager to making me a better presenter. It also made me better with people. And it made me a better crisis manager. All of those things later helped me be a better CEO (once I reached that stage in my career).

But if I hadn't had someone else pushing me into that sales role, I wouldn't have done it. I would not have gained that valuable experience. I had a rigid mindset of who I was and what I wanted to do, and it did not involve being a sales guy like my dad. It took a pivot—someone else kicking my butt to break out of that rigid concept I'd created for myself. And, wow, am I glad they did.

Just as I didn't set out to be in sales, I didn't set out to be a change agent. But when Publicis asked me to revitalize Razorfish Health, I proactively took on the role of storyteller-in-chief in a big way for the first time. At Razorfish, I first tried to incite change with a motivational, top-line, cheerleader-style speech. I showed up in my best suit on the first day and *talked* about how were going to turn the agency around. It was only a few weeks later that I realized it was going to take a lot more than some motivational speeches to make change happen.

That's when I called that off-site meeting I mentioned in the introduction—the one where I assembled thirty-five senior functional leaders and gifted each one a copy of Angela Duckworth's *Grit* and a compass. That's when we came together to be brutally honest, identifying what had to change and how we might change it. It's when we identified the north point on the compass for the Razorfish Health change journey. That job at Razorfish ended up being a way bigger undertaking than I'd anticipated. But it was yet another unanticipated gift—another pivot.

I often tell people that my professional life makes more sense when I look at it backward.

I've experienced the gift of the pivot more than once in my career. In most cases, the "gift" only became apparent in retrospect. I often tell people that my professional life makes more sense when I look at it backward. As I was living through some of these moments, these unprecedented and unexpected changes that were put upon me, I certainly didn't see the sense in them.

When I was sitting on the plane flying to California to head up the West Coast sales team for Roche, I wasn't feeling appreciative or thankful. It was only once I got on the ground in Orange County, once I started the job and began engaging with the role, that I realized, "Hey, wait a minute, this is a real opportunity. I'm adding to my personal toolbox as a professional. This will help me, regardless of how fast it moves me up the corporate ladder."

Now, years later, I can retrace my journey and see how I developed every step of the way. I can identify how every role taught me something, helped shape me, and, ultimately, helped lead me to the next step.

Everybody's journey is their own, and sometimes the journey doesn't make sense until you look back over it later, after some time has passed. I've had plenty of pivots in my career. Some of them I've leaned into proactively; others I've leaned into only with some prodding. The lesson I've learned? We need to trust in the pivot. When things don't go to plan, it can be a gift, not a curse. And that can apply in both personal and professional contexts, I think.

My time at Health Monitor exemplifies that. The COVID-19 pandemic forced the company, and me as a leader, to adapt in ways we had never anticipated or even imagined. Health Monitor went from a legacy print media company to a modern, twenty-first-century, digital-first company. Health Monitor's people found ways to work remotely. And I, as Health Monitor's CEO, adapted my leadership style to the moment. The pandemic certainly made me a more flexible and empathetic leader. Now if you tell me that you want to work two days per week from home in your lululemons, because that's how you're most productive, I'm on board. Pre-COVID-19, I might have been more skeptical.

My experience at Health Monitor is also where I put into practice all those years of development, all those lessons I've picked up in my various roles, from Razorfish to Roche and beyond. It's where my approach to change, to organizational transformation, was put to the ultimate test, thanks to an external force that rocked all our worlds these last years: the COVID-19 pandemic.

Health Monitor was the ultimate test of the three Cs approach, using culture, communication, and competitive advantage to implement meaningful, lasting organizational change.

Again, for me, culture is the most important building block for transformation. It creates the expectations of an organization, defines the values the company will pursue, and sets the stage for all subsequent action. It must be addressed first, before any other part of transformation. Those old business books, from the 1980s and 1990s, may give culture a back seat, focusing instead on points like innovating products and reinvigorating customer relationships. For me, culture deserves a spot in the front—in the driver's seat. Culture, above all else, helps shape and spur on successful change.

Cultural change looks different for different organizations, but there are a few issues I've seen arise again and again in my roles as a change agent. Siloed business operations, cocktail napkin deals, a lack of transparency, general negativity—these are problems I've witnessed repeatedly, at various organizations and in diverse industries. They often need to be dealt with first before true transformation can begin.

Ultimately, cultural change starts with staking out strong values. At Health Monitor, for example, I planted the proverbial flag in the ground for three key values: transparency, initiative, and teamwork. And those values guided all the changes we made as a company, from sharing data about our physician network with our clients' agency partners, to getting rid of the numbered spaces in the corporate parking lot.

It's up to the change agent—the person I like to call the storyteller-in-chief—to communicate and reiterate those values. That brings me to the second C in the process: communication. As a leader, you can't just share your core values in a one-off PowerPoint presentation. You've got to communicate those values honestly, with consistency and clarity, to the people in your organization.

I've discussed some of the ways I did this at Health Monitor, from sending out biweekly update emails to creating monthly CEO videos. We conceptualized those videos as a sort of visual podcast, an ongoing media format that we were always adding to and expanding on. It was important to us to keep the lines of communication open, especially as the company weathered the storm of COVID-19.

Finally, there's the third C, often the driver for a company's desire to change in the first place: competitive advantage. Without the culture and communication components in place, I think it's much harder to maintain competitiveness, especially in the long term. I've pointed to companies that were missing part of the puzzle and suffered as a result. Kodak, for example, failed to embrace the culture of innovation needed to sustain relevancy in the age of digital photography.

A lot of people think that advertising and marketing are what make the competitive advantage. However, I share the viewpoint of P&G CEO Jon R. Moeller: it comes from having an irresistibly superior product. You've got to convince consumers your product or service is so much better than what the other guy has to offer that they will pick your product or service first, every time, without regret, even if it costs more—because they are confident that it is indisputably, undeniably superior. They know that the extra pennies or dollars they spend are worth it, so they spend them happily.

Creating that irresistibly superior product or service starts with the customer. You've got to get obsessed with your customer and stay obsessed with them. What do they want? What do they need? What's the pain point? What problem can you solve for them? What *new* problem can you solve for them? How have their needs and wants evolved? Those are the questions to ask and to keep asking, over and over again.

How you implement those three Cs of culture, communication, and competitive advantage is up to you. Every organization's needs are unique, and you're best positioned to know what will help yours thrive. But, in my experience, regardless of the type of organization or the industry you're working in, there is one last point, a red thread that needs to be inextricably woven into the change process: values and transparency. Without those core components, meaningful *lasting* transformation is difficult, if not downright impossible, to achieve.

Again, the Health Monitor story—and the point-of-care marketing industry at large—is a wonderful testament to that fact. The industry had its moment of reckoning when one organization (no longer active) was publicly taken to task for not having accurately reported its media numbers. In that moment, it was clear that a change was needed.

In response, firms came together to work with POCMA and establish validation and verification standards for media numbers. Those standards are still used today, with audits done by third parties. This assures total confidence in the system. Now any advertising agency or marketer that is utilizing point-of-care media can be sure of the rigorous and reliable reporting, verification, and certification standards applied to those third-party audits.

Throughout its many changes, Health Monitor—a company that's weathered many a storm over its forty-plus years of existence—has always insisted on maintaining strong values. That commitment to ethics has helped inform the company's self-identification as, first and foremost, an educational media company, not a marketing agency. It's informed our high standards for content, which is created by heavily credentialed health journalists in partnership with a bespoke group of medical advisors from some of the most respected educational institutions in the country, from Harvard Medical School to Johns Hopkins and Yale.

It's that commitment to values and transparency that has, in turn, allowed Health Monitor to place its educational materials not only in the physician's waiting room but also in the exam room, the sacrosanct space where doctor and patient meet. We want to continue to be in the room where it happens. As a Hamilton College alum, I'm partial to *Hamilton*, and I often think of Alexander Hamilton and his insistence on being in the drawing room with George Washington. He insisted on being part of the conversation. And Health Monitor wants to continue to be part of the conversation too—in this case, the conversation that takes place between doctor and patient, the real heroes of healthcare.

Values and transparency help create changes with lasting impact. They help build companies with longevity. And, as I've said, living a life, personally and professionally, built on values and transparency is also simply *the right thing to do*. Again, a lot of life is gray, but ethics are, in my world, black and white.

In a change journey, values and transparency gain even greater significance. They help you find your north point on the compass, and they help you stay the course. This is especially important because transformation can, at times, be chaotic. This is especially true when it's carried out quickly, which it often is.

Successful transformation often requires great urgency. For the storyteller-in-chief, it usually demands fast decision-making. That's where that one-way door versus two-way door policy I mentioned comes into play: if a decision can be undone, if you can walk through the door both ways, make it fast. If it's a one-way door decision that can't be undone, like firing someone, give it the consideration it's due.

As a storyteller-in-chief, you also want to make sure you're sur-rounding yourself with people who share your commitment to values and transparency. Because change doesn't come from one person. It requires the effort of many. The storyteller-in-chief may be leading the marathon, but they need their pacemakers or pacesetters, the people who run alongside them, helping them to maintain momentum and providing psychological support.

To build that team, you've got to empower people at every level. You have to give your leadership team the personal agency to make decisions and take action. And that has to trickle down, as your leadership team has to allow the people that *they* work with every day to take initiative without fear of reprisal.

Change is tough, and organizational change in particular is a momentous undertaking, requiring attention to everything from products to processes and people. You don't want to go it alone. When I think of the change journeys I've overseen, I know for a fact that I could not have accomplished them without the help of others. I've been fortunate enough to have many talented people accompany me on each of my change journeys, every step of the way.

When I started this book, I told you that it wasn't a concrete guidebook for change. It's not. There is no one formula for successful transformation, because every person's and every company's situation is unique. However, in my experience, there are a few building blocks that help make successful change possible: culture, communication,

Nine times out of ten, you aren't *actually* stuck.

and competitive advantage. And it takes great people, people who are committed to the same values and transparency as the storyteller-in-chief, to put those building blocks into place.

Those people are also going to be there in the moments when you, the person driving transformation, feel stuck. Inevitably, in a transformation journey, you will hit walls. You will face hurdles. You will lose momentum. You will start to feel uncomfortably *stuck*. And that can leave you demotivated, wondering if you're really going to be able to accomplish what you've set out to do.

So often people shy away from change or avoid transformation because they feel *stuck*. Here's one last secret I'll let you in on, something that took me years to learn: nine times out of ten, you aren't *actually* stuck.

Yes, there are certain situations in life that you cannot change. Some life-or-death matters are beyond your control (or anyone else's). I've faced a few of those situations, following the deaths of my parents and my wife. And those situations where you have no control are among the most humbling and scary any human being must face.

But, those terrible instances aside, I honestly believe that we as people *can* change most of the situations we're put in. There is the 10 percent you can't control, those life-or-death moments. The other 90 percent? I think you can change it. Whether it's the bad job, the bad boss, or the bad significant other, you're not stuck in those situations. You've got the power to swing the boom and change the direction of the ship, to go and do something different. You can reposition the job, change your boss, or pack your bags and leave your partner (I'm not saying you *should* necessarily—but just that you *can*).

Whatever the situation may be, there is likely a pivot that's possible. Again, there is the exception, the handful of situations that you can't change. If someone passes away, you can't undo that. On a lighter note, hey, I'd love to be six foot three. Guess what: it's not happening. I'm a grown man. Six foot three isn't in the cards for me. But those other things? Your job, your partner, your city, your school? You can change them.

Again, making those changes is a lot easier with some support. When I was younger, I was too stubborn to make changes in my career that needed to be made. At Roche, someone else pointed my ship in a different direction *for me* by booting me from marketing to sales. It took someone older and wiser than me to say, "Hey, it's great that you love marketing, but you should really learn about the sales side of things too. Because if you're going to be a leader, a CEO, you've got to gain that perspective." And they were right. Now, looking back, I'm extremely grateful for that pivot—even if I wasn't grateful at the time.

And that's not the only pivot that's been thrust upon me. I didn't ask to be a sales guy. I didn't ask to be a change agent. I didn't even ask to be in pharmaceuticals, originally—when I first landed at P&G, I was desperate to work in their consumer goods division, and I wasn't exactly thrilled when they stuck me in pharma. Now, decades later, I'm thankful that they started me in pharmaceuticals and that that's where I stayed.

Those pivots were all gifts. I can see that now, even if I didn't then. And that's the lesson that I've learned, often through some hardship, that I hope to pass on. Yes, change can be scary. But you shouldn't be afraid of it, and you certainly shouldn't shy away from it. Learning to embrace the pivots will, I promise you, make life so much better.

The world is changing, faster than ever, and the people (and companies) who learn how to change with it are the ones that will thrive. Those that don't—well, they'll join the ranks of Kodak and Blackberry. Like those companies, they may not disappear completely, but they also won't be at the top of their field.

If you walk away from this book with anything, I hope that it's with an appreciation for the gift of the pivot. I hope you can start to see how sometimes those scary changes, the ones we least expect, are the ones that do the most for us in life. People can change. Companies can change. Relationships can change. Everything in life is about being able to make pivots, to evolve.

If you have the opportunity to take something good and make it better, don't let fear hold you back. I started my life as a rule player. I was the guy who wanted to go the Naval Academy. I was the Senator, diplomatically staking out both sides of any argument.

Now I'm less rigid about following the rules. I'm not so intent on coloring inside the lines. And I'm better for it. But it took some hardships to get me here. And, in many cases—as with Roche—it took the guidance and encouragement of other people to set me and my ship on the right course.

That is something I want to pay forward. I think we all benefit from positive change, and I think we all deserve to have both the knowledge and the confidence needed to make change. This book is one small way I hope I can help, by giving you some of the tools—and the encouragement—to enact change and become your own storyteller-in-chief, whether it's in your personal or your professional life.

ACKNOWLEDGMENTS

I want to thank the following people as part of *Coming About*:

- Banafsheh Pirasteh Paragamian, my wife and partner

- My three children, Emily, Melissa, Matthew

- The Health Monitor senior leadership team: Donna Barker, Steve Blahut, Augie Caruso, Kristy Chipley, Rob Dougherty, Howard Halligan, Erica Kerber, Maria Lissandrello, Will Saint-Louis, Keith Sedlak, Dan Tassone, Kim Vivas, Dawn Veziran

- Rick Williams of WestView Capital Partners

- Alison Kilian

Some of the great leaders I have had the opportunity to work with and for:

- Tom Finn, CEO of Procter & Gamble Healthcare, retired

- Hal Russo

- Ed Mitzen, CEO of the Fingerpaint Group

- Donna Murphy, CEO of Havas Health & You

- Neil Matheson, Board Chair, Atlantis Healthcare

- Tom Watlington

- The former Roche Diagnostics sales leadership team: Bob Hazelet, Dan Kane (posthumously), Regan Lombardo, Jim Rowen, Tony Schott, Brad Shelton

CPSIA information can be obtained
at www.ICGtesting.com
Printed in the USA
BVHW040803220523
664629BV00012B/399/J